ARIEH HANDLER

Modest
Jewish Hero

A tribute by Aubrey Rose

Lennard Publishing

This edition first published in the UK in 2010
by Lennard Publishing
a division of Lennard Associates Ltd
Windmill Cottage
Mackerye End
Harpenden
Herts AL5 5DR

ISBN 978 1 85291 151 5

A catalogue entry is available from the British Library.

Printed and bound in the UK
by Butler Tanner & Dennis

CONTENTS

GLOSSARY

HEBREW NAMES

Since Hebrew writing follows its own ancient alphabet, there is more than one correct way of transcribing Hebrew words into English.

Aliyah
Literally: 'going up' or 'ascent'. Jewish immigration to Israel. A legal right under Israel's Law of Return for Jews all over the world. Includes both voluntary immigration for ideological, emotional, or practical reasons and, on the other hand, mass flight of persecuted populations of Jews.

Ashkenazi
A broad term for European Jews, traditionally refers to Jews descended from the medieval Jewish communities.

Chalutz (Chalutzim)
Literally: 'pioneer(s)'. Usually denotes the Jewish settlers who arrived in Palestine between 1882 and 1935.

Chassid
Literally: 'pious person'. Today generally denotes one who is a member of the Chassidim.

Chassidim
Ultra-orthodox Ashkenazi Jews belonging to the movement founded in eastern Europe by the Baal Shem Tov in the 18th Century. A religious and social movement to this day.

Chaverim
Friends or close colleagues.

Chumash
The Five Books of Moses, also known as the Pentateuch or Torah. The word comes from the Hebrew word for five, chamesh.

Eretz Yisrael
The 'land of Israel'.

Exodus
A ship that carried 4,500 European Jews, mostly Holocaust survivors, to British mandated Palestine in 1947. The ship was turned back upon arrival at Haifa causing great controversy. The second book of the Chumash.

Falashas
A name given to the Jews of Ethiopia, who call themselves Beta Israel (house of Israel). Many Falashas made aliyah, most notably during Operation Moses 1984 and Operation Solomon 1991.

Falash Mura	*A group of Ethiopian Jews who abandoned their faith yet deem to be entitled to Israeli citizenship on the strength of Jewish descent/blood lines.*
Hachshara	*Literally: 'Preparation'. Specifically, hachshara includes all forms of personal and ideological development, experience and training for immigration to Israel.*
Kashrut	*Refers to Jewish dietary laws. Food in accord with halacha (Jewish law) is termed kosher meaning fit to eat. Kashrut as a term broadly covers all of the specific laws relating to ritual slaughter, cooking and preparing foods, and which foods are acceptable.*
Kibbutz (Kibbutzim)	*Collective community(ies) in Israel that were traditionally based on agriculture. The kibbutz is a form of communal living that combines socialism and Zionism.*
Kibbutznik	*A person who lives and works on a Kibbutz.*
Kippa	*A skull-cap. A ritual head covering worn mostly by Jewish males, particularly during prayer.*
Limmud	*Literally: 'learning'.*
Mishnah	*The Mishnah is considered to be the first important work of Rabbinic Judaism, and is the first legal compendium of oral Torah traditions, dating from the early third century CE, and including material from the previous two centuries. Presents cases, presenting both the debate and judgment where rabbis have interpreted laws from the Torah to be applicable to everyday life.*
Mishnaic	*Traditions dating from the time of the Mishnah (70 - 200 CE approx).*
Refusenik	*"One who is not allowed to perform aliyah". An unofficial term for individuals, typically but not exclusively Soviet Jews, who were denied permission to emigrate abroad by the authorities of the former Soviet Union.*

Semichah   *The ordination of a rabbi, often accompanied by relevant certification from various rabbinic authorities.*

Sephardi   *Jews who originated in the Iberian Peninsula. This classification now includes Jews who follow the customs of Iberian and Eastern Jews.*

Shaliach   *Emissary. Member of the Yishuv during the mandate period sent to assist and advise Diaspora Jews in connection with aliyah. Today extended to aid in Jewish education.*

Siddur(im)   *Jewish Prayer book(s), containing the set order of daily prayers, and psalms and prayers for special occasions.*

Talmud   *A record of rabbinic discussions pertaining to Jewish law, ethics, customs, and history based on the Mishnah. It is a central text of mainstream Judaism.*

Torah   *The founding religious document of Judaism, comprising the five books of Moses. Most Jews believe that the Torah is of Divine origin.*

Yeshiva   *Originating in the third century and still numerous today, yeshivas or yeshivot are Rabbinic schools/academies for advanced study in Torah, Mishnah and Talmud.*

Yiddish   *A Germanic hybrid language spoken by Jews of the Rhineland from the 10th Century. The language spread and was the dominant language spoken by Ashkenazi Jews in Eastern Europe. Yiddish survives currently and is still taught to schoolchildren particularly amongst the ultra-orthodox communities.*

Zionism   *A word used to denote a yearning of the Jewish people, as contained in their prayers, for their homeland. In the modern usage, appearing at the end of the 19th century, it denotes a movement whose goal is the return of the Jewish people to Israel.*

Zohar   *The Zohar first appeared in Spain in the 13th century. The central work in the Kabbalah, a mystical commentary on the Bible. It is attributed to Rabbi Simeon bar Yohai, who lived in the 2nd century CE.*

INDIVIDUALS

Stanley Abramovich *Member of Bachad. Senior official of Joint Distribution Committee, Israel*

Akavya ben Mehalalel *(First Century CE). Member of the Sanhedrin, famous scholar who refused to renounce four of his decisions with which the majority disagreed, forfeiting the position of leader of the Beth Din. Famous for his maxim 'Know from where you have come and whither you are bound and before whom you are destined to give account' (Avot 3:1).*

Chaim Arlosoroff *Head of Political Department of the Jewish Agency from 1931 to 1933.*

Baal Shem Tov *(1698 - 1760). Rabbi Yisroel (Israel) ben Eliezer known as Baal Shem Tov (Master of the Good Name) or Besht, born in Okopy formerly in Poland, now Ukraine, was a Jewish mystical rabbi who has numerous miracles attributed to him. He is the founder of Chassidism. Revered as one of the great Chassidim.*

Rabbi Leo Baeck *(1873 - 1956). German Rabbi who studied at the University of Berlin as well as receiving theological training. From 1933 President of the Reichsvertretung, the representative body of German Jews. Chairman of the World Union for Progressive Judaism from 1948 until his death.*

Dr. Aharon Barth *(1890 - 1957). Born in Berlin, an active leader of the Mizrachi movement in Germany, Chairman of the Zionist Congress court from 1946. Moved to Palestine 1933, appointed director-general of Bank Leumi in 1947 until his death.*

Menachem Begin *(1913 - 1992). Israeli former Prime Minister and statesman serving in the first to the tenth Knessets, Born in Brest Litovsk, he led 'armed warfare' against the British in Palestine in 1944. Won his first general election as head of Likud in 1977. Especially known for signing Israel's peace treaty with Egypt in 1979.*

David Ben-Gurion *(1886 - 1973). Israeli statesman and the first Prime Minister of Israel (1948 - 1953 and 1955 - 1963), who dedicated his life to establishing a Jewish homeland in Palestine and was regarded by many as the father of his country.*

Professor Norman Bentwich *(1883 - 1971). Lawyer and scholar. Born in London, moved to Palestine via Cairo. 1920 - 1931 Attorney General of the Mandate Government in Palestine and a major legal reformer. Resigned 1931 and became a prolific scholar and writer.*

Tony Blair *(b 1953). Politician, Labour, Prime Minister of Great Britain 1997 - 2007. Later EU special envoy to the Middle East.*

Yosef Burg *(1909 - 1999). Rabbi, Dr., born Dresden, Germany. Israeli politician, leader of the National Religious Party.*
Active in the Mizrachi movement, moved to Eretz Yisrael 1939, Member of the Zionist Council as head of Youth Aliyah until 1940. Held various posts in the Knesset from 1949, and Government Minister.

Sarah Churchill *(1914 - 1982). Later Baroness Audley, second daughter of Prime Minister Winston Churchill. Actress and artist.*

Adolf Eichmann *(1906 - 1962). Prominent Nazi, SS Lieutenant-Colonel, active in implementing and organiser of the Holocaust, later captured by Israeli agents and tried and convicted in Israel. Remains the only individual to have been executed under Israeli law.*

Albert Einstein *(1879 - 1955). Jewish German-born American physicist and Nobel Laureate, best known as the creator of the special and general theories of relativity and for his bold hypothesis concerning the particle nature of light. Time Magazine's 'Person of The Century' for the 20th Century.*

Rabbi Dr. Isidore Epstein
(1894 - 1962). Born in Kovni, Lithuania. Principal of Jews College, prominently involved in the first English translation of the Babylonian Talmud. Famous for his book 'Faith of Judaism' published 1954 which attracted much favourable attention.

Israel Finestein Q.C.
(1921 - 2009). British judge, historian and communal leader. President of the Board of Deputies of British Jews 1991 - 1994 and a noted writer on Anglo-Jewish history.

Lord Samuel Fisher
President of Board of Deputies, and prominent ally of Arieh in the campaign for Soviet and Ethiopian Jews. Held numerous offices in Anglo-Jewry.

Rabbi Fishman
Later known as Rabbi Maimon in Israel. Signed the Declaration of Independence. Leader of Religious Zionist Movement. First Minister of Religious Affairs.

Recha Frier
(1892 - 1984). Born in Norden, Ostfriesland Germany, conceived the idea of Youth Aliyah and ran the programme leaving Germany for Israel in 1940. She won the Israel Prize in 1981.

Colonel Gaddafi
(b 1942 - aka Muammar Abu Minyar al-Gaddafi). De facto leader of Libya since 1969.

Mikhail Gorbachev
(b 1931). Russian politician. General Secretary of the Communist Party from 1985 until 1991, and the last head of state of the USSR, serving from 1988 until its collapse in 1991.

Danny Handler
(b 1944). Son of Arieh.

Ephraim Handler
(1881 - 1951). Father of Arieh.

Gaby Handler
(b 1946). Son of Arieh.

Helena Handler (née Schönwetter)
(1886 - 1967). Mother of Arieh.

**Henny Handler
(née Prilutzky)** *(1919 - 2007). Wife of Arieh.*

Julius Handler *(1910 - 1990). Brother of Arieh.*

Moritz Handler *(1909 - 1971). Brother of Arieh.*

Hans Heinemann *A teacher at the Manchester Merkaz Limmud and author of 'Torah and the Social Order'.*

Lady Henriques *(1889 - 1972). Lady Rosa Louise. A noted social worker, chairwoman of the German section of Jewish Relief Abroad. Wife of Sir Basil Lucas Henriques.*

**Chief Rabbi
Joseph Hertz** *(1872 - 1946). Elected to be Chief Rabbi of United Hebrew Congregations of the British Empire Great Britain and the Commonwealth in 1913. Prominent Zionist advocate. Made Companion of Honour (CH) in 1943, first rabbi to receive the honour.*

Theodor Herzl *(1860 - 1904). Theodor (Binyamin Ze'ev) Herzl, the visionary of Zionism, was born in Budapest in 1860. His experiences whilst working as a journalist in Paris during the Dreyfus Trial led him to pursue the goal of a state for Jews. Published 'Der Judenstaat' (The Jewish State, 1896), he was later elected as the first President of the World Zionist Organisation and worked tirelessly appealing to world leaders on behalf of the Zionist cause.*

**Chaim (Vivian)
Herzog** *(1918 - 1997). Son of Chief Rabbi Herzog. Served as Israeli Ambassador to the UN (1975 - 1978) and as the sixth President of Israel (1983 - 1993) following a distinguished career in both the British Army and the Israel Defence Forces.*

Yaakov Herzog *(1921 - 1972). Son of Chief Rabbi Herzog. Rabbi, legal scholar, lawyer, and doctor of international law he published translations and commentary of several tracts of the Mishnah., Advisor to Ben-Gurion and Israeli Ambassador to Canada. Was prospective Chief Rabbi, but died young.*

Rabbi Dr. Azriel Hildesheimer
(1820 - 1899). German Rabbi, scholar and leader of Orthodox Jewry. Considered by some to be the father of Modern Orthodoxy. In 1864 published a declaration recognising the Jewishness of Ethiopian Jewry (republished by M. Waldman, Sinai 95).

Rabbi Hillel
(circa first Century BCE). Hillel, called the Elder (the title "Rabbi" was not used for him or his contemporaries in Talmudic sources). Famous Mishnaic sage and teacher. Founder of school of Hillel. Noted for his humility and tolerance. Born in Babylon, studied and taught in Jerusalem.

Lord Desmond Hirshfield
(1913 - 1993). (Desmond Barel). Was created Baron Hirshfield, of Holborn in Greater London on 30 August 1967. Served as honorary treasurer of the Jewish Agricultural Committee.

King Hussein of Jordan
(1935 - 1999). King of Jordan for 46 years from 1952 - 1999. In 1994 he concluded negotiations to end the official state of war with Israel resulting in the Israel Jordan Treaty of Peace.

Rabbi Dr. Louis Jacobs
(1920 - 2006). Founding Rabbi of the UK Masorti movement, formerly Rabbi of the New London Synagogue, author of 'We Have Reason to Believe', and other scholarly works. Formerly Rabbi of New West End Synagogue in London.

Lady Jakobovits
(1928 - 2010). née Amélie Munk. Wife of late Chief Rabbi Lord Jakobovits.

Lord Barnett Janner
(1892 - 1982). British politician, Zionist and communal leader. Both Liberal and Labour Member of Parliament from 1931 - 1970. President of the Zionist Federation of Great Britain 1950 and Board of Deputies 1955 - 1964. Knighted in 1965 and made a life peer 1970.

Lord Greville Janner Q.C. *(b 1928). British politician in the Labour Party. He represented Leicester North West and then Leicester West in the House of Commons from 1970 until his retirement in 1997. President of the Board of Deputies of British Jews from 1978 to 1984 and named a life peer in 1997.*

David Kessler *(1906 - 1999). OBE, born in Pretoria, Chairman and Managing Director of The Jewish Chronicle for 50 years. Author of 'The Falashas: the forgotten Jews of Ethiopia', published in 1982.*

Chief Rabbi Kook *(1865 - 1935). The first Ashkenazi chief rabbi for Palestine, the founder of the Religious Zionist Yeshiva Merkaz HaRav, Jewish hinker, Halachist, Kabbalist and a renowned Torah scholar.*

Akiva Levinsky *Jewish Agency Treasurer.*

Alex Margulies *Key supporter of the Jewish Agricultural Committee and Member of the National Council for Soviet Jewry.*

Shalom Markovitch (Maagan) *One of the founders of Kibbutz Lavi.*

Golda Meir *(1898 - 1978). Born in Kiev, politician, was the fourth Prime Minister of Israel. After a youth in Kiev and USA, she moved to join a Kibbutz and became an increasingly dedicated Labour Zionist. She signed the Israeli Declaration of Independence and served in key political positions at various times, including Ambassador to Moscow, Labour Minster and Foreign Minister.*

Field Marshal Montgomery *(1887 - 1976). Anglo-Irish British Army officer. He successfully commanded Allied forces during the Second World War, known especially for successfully commanding troops at the Battle of El Alamein.*

Benno Penner *A close friend of Arieh's. Born in Glasgow he cared for and organised the Jews who were held up in Cyprus on their way to Israel.*

13

Shimon Peres *(b 1923). Born in Wiszniewo, in Poland (now Belarus), President of the State of Israel. Moved with his family to Palestine in 1934. Has held numerous posts in government representing five political parties in a political career which began in 1952. Awarded the Nobel Peace Prize in 1994 for his part in the Oslo peace agreements.*

Rivka Prilutzky *(1886 - 1963). Mother of Henny Handler, Arieh's wife. Escaped from Berlin and spent the remainder of the war in Paris. In 1945 she boarded the first boat to Palestine.*

Yitzhak Prilutzky *(1876 - 1942). Henny's father, perished in Auschwitz.*

Yitzhak Rabin *(1922 - 1995). Prime Minister of Israel 1974 - 1977 and 1992 until his assassination in 1995, he also served as Israel Defence Force Chief of Staff during the Six Day War and later as Defence Minister. He was awarded the Nobel Peace Prize in 1994 for his role in the Oslo Accords.*

Tibor (Pinchas) Rosenbaum *Rabbi Dr. risked his life saving Jews in Hungary. Founded Geneva-based International Credit Bank.*

Arthur Ruppin *(1876 - 1943). Born in Rawicz in the German Empire (today in Poland). Zionist thinker and leader. He was also one of the founders of the city of Tel Aviv, and a pioneering sociologist credited as being "The Father Of Jewish Sociology".*

C.P. Scott *(1846 - 1932). Journalist, publisher and politician. Born in Bath, Somerset, he was the editor of the Manchester Guardian from 1872 until 1929 and its owner from 1907 until his death. He was also a Liberal Member of Parliament and pursued a similarly liberal agenda as an editor.*

Emperor Haile Selassie *(1892 - 1975). Born Tafari Makonnen, was Ethiopia's regent from 1916 to 1930 and Emperor of Ethiopia from 1930 to 1974.*

Enzio Sereni *(1905 - 1944). Italian Zionist, co-founder of kibbutz Givat Brenner, scholar, advocate of Jewish-Arab co-existence and a resistance fighter who was parachuted into Nazi-occupied Italy in the Second World War.*

14

Anatole Sharansky
(b 1948). Now known as Natan. A notable former Soviet dissident, Human Rights activist, former 'Prisoner of Zion'. A focal point for refusenik activities, after release in 1986. He is a well-regarded politician and author in Israel. Head of Jewish Agency. Married to Avital Sharansky.

Moshe Sharett
(1894 - 1965). Prominent Zionist and Prime Minister of Israel 1954 - 1955. Head of the Political department of the World Zionist Organisation from 1933 - 1948.

Zalman Shragai
(1899 - 1995). Religious Zionist Leader. Born in Gorzkowice, Poland, A founder of the Mizrachi movement in Poland, he settled in Palestine in 1924. Elected Mayor of Jerusalem 1950 - 1952.

Hayim Solomon
Signatory of the American Declaration of Independence 1776.

Rabbi Dr. Soloveichek
(1903 - 1993). Joseph Dov. Talmudist and Philosopher. Orthodox leader. Born in Poland lived in Boston, USA.

Rabbi Shmuel Sperber
A teacher at the Manchester Merkaz Limmud. Rabbinic authority of Bachad, UK.

Susan Sperber
Arieh's secretary at Bachad Fellowship.

Sir Sigmund Sternberg
Notable figure in World Interfaith organisations. Member of the National Council for Soviet Jewry . Founder of Three Faiths Forum.

Rabbi Susya
Famous Chassid. 18th Century.

Henrietta Szold
(1860 - 1945). US Zionist leader. Founder of the Women's Zionist Movement, Hadassah, settled in Palestine 1920 from where she led her organisation and also from 1933 Youth Aliyah. Sent Arieh to UK in 1935.

Margaret Thatcher *(b 1925). Politician, Conservative, Prime Minister of Great Britain 1979 - 1990. Elected for an unprecedented three terms, also the only woman to have held the post in Great Britain. She holds a life peerage as Baroness Thatcher of Kesteven.*

Henny Ungar *(1911 - 1981). Sister of Arieh.*

Moshe Unna *One of a few Jews who came from Palestine to Germany in the early 1930s to train Jews in agriculture and leadership. Member of Knesset. Leader of the Religious Zionist Movement. Lived in Kibbutz Sde Eliyahu.*

Chief Rabbi Issar Yehuda Unterman *(1886 - 1976). Born in Belorussia, moved to England and was appointed Rabbi of Liverpool in 1924. President of the British Mizrachi organisation. Later Ashkenazi Chief Rabbi of Israel.*

Dr. Chaim Weizmann *(1874 - 1952). Scientist, Zionist leader, President of the World Zionist Organisation, and the first President of the State of Israel. He was elected on 1 February 1949, and served until his death in 1952.*

Harold Wilson *(1916 - 1995). Labour politician, Prime Minister of the United Kingdom from 1964 to 1970, and again from 1974 to 1976. The most recent British Prime Minister to serve non-consecutive terms.*

Chief Rabbi Ovadia Yosef *(b 1920). Born in Baghdad Iraq, elected Sephardi Chief Rabbi of Israel in 1972. The spiritual leader of the Shas ultra-orthodox political party in Israel.*

ORGANISATIONS

American Joint
Distribution
Committee   *(est. 1914). Founded to alleviate famine for Palestinian Jews it has continued in its mission to aid Jews in distress around the world. Now offers support to Jews and non-Jews alike.*

Association of
Jewish Refugees   *A group that provides an extensive range of social and welfare services, and grants financial assistance to Jewish victims of Nazi persecution living in Great Britain.*

Bachad   *League of Religious Pioneers. Before the Second World War there existed a religious Zionist youth movement in Germany called Brit Chalutzim Dattiyim, - shortened to its initial letters Bachad. Its members prepared themselves for aliyah. A group of them came over to England among the refugees who were permitted to enter this country in the years immediately before the war. Arieh established Bachad in the UK in 1939. The Bachad Fellowship continues to support the work of Bnei Akiva today.*

Bank Leumi   *(est. 1902). An Israeli bank. It was founded in London as the Anglo Palestine Company and was conceived by Theodore Herzl.*

Bnei Akiva   *Founded in Palestine in the 1920s and established in 1939 in the UK by Arieh. The largest religious Zionist youth movement in the world, educates young people in the ideals of religious Zionism and Torah study.*

Board of Deputies
of British Jews   *Founded in 1760, as a joint committee of Sephardi and Ashkenazi Jews in London. Widely recognised as the elected representative body of the UK Jewish community.*

Brit Hanoar
Youth Group   *(est. 1926) A non-religious and non-political youth organisation whose primary aim was to improve wages and working conditions for young people in Palestine. With 100,000 members in 1970, the group expanded its remit to include, camps, daily meetings and co-operative living.*

Central British
Fund (CBF)   *(est. 1933). Played a major role in organising the Kindertransport which brought 70,000 Jewish people to safety before the start of the Second World War. Now World Jewish Relief (WJR).*

Chovevei Zion   *Also known as Chibbat Zion, (Those who love Zion). Refers to supporters of settlement in Eretz Yisrael preceding the establishment of the modern Zionist movement.*

Falasha Welfare
Association   *(est. 1972). A group set up to assist the Jews of Ethiopia and campaign for their transfer to Israel.*

Gestapo   *Contraction of* Geheime Staatspolizei, *translates as 'Secret State Police'. Was the official secret police of Nazi Germany; under the overall administration of the* Schutzstaffel *(SS) among whom Adolf Eichmann was prominent.*

Haganah   *(est. 1920). Jewish defence force, active in British mandated Palestine. A precursor of the Israel Defence Force.*

Hapoel
Hamizrachi   *(est. 1922). A political party and settlement movement that supported the founding of religious kibbutzim and moshavim. One of the predecessors of the modern-day National Religious Party.*

International
Credit Bank   *A Geneva-based bank which gathered the contributions of Jews in Europe and the Americas and invested them in Israel in the 1950s and elsewhere.*

Jewish Agency — *Recognised during the British mandate as the main political representative of the Jewish people on all matters relating to the establishment of a Jewish National Homeland in Palestine.*

Jewish Agricultural Committee — *(est. 1939). A group set up by Arieh to support Bachad. Desmond Hirshfield, Oscar Phillips, Rebecca Sieff, Elaine Laski and Norman Bentwich were involved.*

Keren Kayemet Le Yisrael (later JNF) — *(est. 1901). A non-profit organisation dedicated to development and improvement of Israel through afforestation, water conservation, ecology and educational activities.*

Kibbutz Lavi — *(est. 1949). Lavi (Lion) is a kibbutz in the Lower Galilee area of Israel. It is a member of the Religious Kibbutz Movement which Arieh helped to found.*

Likud — *(est. 1973). The major centre-right political party in Israel. The alliance of several right-wing parties.*

Merkaz Limmud — *A religious teaching establishment set up in Manchester during the Second World War, members came from various leadership training centres for periods of three or six months for intensive Jewish studies.*

National Council for Soviet Jewry — *(est. 1975). A group of British Jews who campaigned against the conditions for Jews in the USSR, particularly for the release of Anatole (later Natan) Sharansky, and for the right of Soviet Jews to emigrate.*

National Council of the Yishuv — *(Hebrew: Va'ad Leumi). Organisation which had grown up on a voluntary basis among the Jews in Palestine to represent the Yishuv.*

Radziner Chassidim
(Radzyn)   *A certain dynasty of Chassidim originating from Radzyn in Poland, famous for using a blue thread in their zizit (prayer shawl fringes) they follow the teachings of Gershon Hanokh Leiner.*

SS   *Active 1923 - 1945 Schutzstaffel abbreviated SS. German for 'Protective Squadron'. Built upon the Nazi racial ideology, these elite paramilitaries were responsible for many of the crimes against humanity perpetrated by the Nazis during the Second World War.*

World Zionist
Congress   *(First held 1897 Basle, Switzerland). The Congress met regularly until 1946. Their goal was to build an infrastructure to further the cause of Jewish settlement in Palestine. Since the foundation of the state, WZC has met every four or five years in Jerusalem.*

Yishuv   *The body of Jewish residents in Eretz Yisrael before the establishment of the State of Israel.*

Youth Aliyah   *(est. 1934). An organisation which saved tens of thousands of young Jews from the Nazis during the Third Reich, arranging for their resettlement in Palestine in kibbutzim and youth villages.*

Zionist Actions
Committee   *Committee elected to run the affairs of the World Zionist Congress between Congresses.*

Zionist General
Council   *The supreme institution of the Zionist movement in the inter-Congress period. Highly influential in the early days of the State of Israel.*

FOREWORD

There was an astonishing moment at the Yom Ha-Aztmaut service, in London, for Israel's 61st birthday. It coincided with the seventieth birthday of Bnei Akiva in Britain, founded in the dark days of 1939.

With a shock of realisation we recalled the fact that it had been Arieh Handler, still alive, still well, still an inspiration to all of us, who had been responsible for that foundation. Moshe Rabbenu led the Jewish people for forty years. Arieh had been a leader for seventy - and more, for even before he founded Bachad he had done outstanding and dangerous work helping Jews escape from Germany.

Arieh was never afraid of danger, and somehow Hashem protected him from harm.

Which of us privileged to be there will ever forget the Bnei Akiva National Weekend in Wales some years ago? It was Friday night, there were almost a thousand young people in the hall, and it was freezing. I said to Arieh, then in his late eighties, "You are the youngest person in the room. Stand up on your chair and start singing, and everyone will join in". Arieh did, I joined him, and together we started singing Shlomo Carlebach's *Gesher Tsar Meod*. Within moments, the entire room had followed suit. Everyone was standing on their chairs, singing at the top of their voices.

The policemen from the Welsh constabulary, who were providing security, heard the noise and feared some terrible mishap. They rushed in, saw everyone singing, and one of them said, "Never before have I seen such exuberance in the absence of alcohol". The next time we held the National Weekend, the police who had been there especially asked to be assigned the same duty because they had enjoyed it so much the first time.

That was, and still is, Arieh Handler, the legend, the role model, the exemplar of all that was and is best in religious Zionism, now breathing the special air of Yerushalayim, the place that always was his spiritual home.

When he celebrated his ninetieth birthday I quoted the description of Moshe Rabbenu at the age of 120: "his vision was undimmed and his natural energy unabated". Until now, I told Arieh, I thought these were just two descriptions, but from you I have learned that the first is the explanation of the second. Moshe's natural energy was unabated because his vision was undimmed, because he never lost the ideals of his youth.

The same is true of Arieh. He dreamed the prophetic dream of Shivat Tziyon, and never lost it in all the years. Even today his spirit is still young, and still an inspiration to me personally and to all who have been privileged to know him and count him as a leader and friend.

May Hashem continue to bless you, Arieh, and may you long continue to be a blessing to us, to Israel and to the Jewish people.

Chief Rabbi Lord Jonathan Sacks

INTRODUCTION

Arieh Handler is a remarkable man, whose story sheds considerable light on several major aspects of recent Jewish history. In Nazi Germany, before the war, he played a leading and courageous part in facilitating the emigration of Jews. In the 1970s, when I came to know him, he was one of the most determined activists in the movement to secure the freedom of Soviet Jews then trapped in the Soviet Union. His devotion to Jewish and Zionist causes, his high sense of responsibility for his fellow Jews, and his high ethical standards, have inspired generations of those who have seen him at work.

In 1948 he was one of those invited to witness the Declaration of Israel's Independence at Tel Aviv; by 2006 he was one of the few remaining to have been present at that historical occasion. That year he decided to leave England for a new life in Israel. On arriving he found not only the enormous Russian Jewish immigrant community that he himself had played a leading role in creating, but also a vibrant community of Ethiopian Jews, whose emigration to Israel had been one of the causes for which he had fought.

Organisationally, Arieh Handler's life spans a remarkable range. He was one of the creators, in 1938, of the Zionist Youth Movement, Bnei Akiva, and has served on the executive of the United Synagogue, the World Zionist Organisation and Jewish Childs Day. No one who has met Arieh Handler, or studied his work, or who reads this book, will be in any doubt as to his remarkable character and achievements.

Sir Martin Gilbert PC, CBE, D. Litt.

Chapter 1

ARIEH - HIS STORY

On 14th May 1948, a short, sturdy man rose in a crowded hall and began to read. Those present held their breath as the speaker announced, "we therefore declare the creation of a State to be called Israel". The speaker was David Ben-Gurion, born in Poland, who had devoted his life to the cause of his people. The place was a handsome building, a museum, in Tel Aviv, a buoyant city that, 40 years earlier, had been but a sand dune.

Among those invited to the ceremony was another short, sturdy individual, one Arieh Handler, born in Brno, Czechoslovakia in 1915, but raised in Magdeburg, Germany, another man who, in his own way, had likewise devoted his life to his people.

Both men, and all present on this historic occasion, may have reflected on the similarity with the birth of another state, far away, the United States of America. In 1776, a Jew, Hayim Solomon, had been amongst those who signed America's Declaration of Independence. Both new states had to fight tenaciously for their freedom. Both emerged from the military control of Great Britain, yet there was a major difference.

The United States was an entirely new concept. The State of Israel was the third independent Jewish Commonwealth in the Holy Land, the first 3000 years earlier, the second over 2000 years before, in the 2nd century BCE, reflecting the hope and prayers over the ages.

As Ben-Gurion read on, and Arieh Handler listened, they may have heard the silent echoes of Jewish history. This was the land of the Biblical prophets, who preached universal values and principles, the land of milk and honey, God-given, where people, in ancient days, struggled with themselves, with divine injunctions, with ever-present threats, indeed hostility, from surrounding empires.

A yet more recent echo, a terrible reverberation, a nightmare, may also have rung in their consciousness. Ben-Gurion had emerged from Poland in 1906, a country where millions of his fellow-Jews had been decimated and burned. Arieh had spent his boyhood and youth in Germany, an advanced nation that had sunk into organised barbarism, culminating in the unique blasphemy of the Holocaust.

Just as the new State reflected one crucial aspect of the rescue of the Jewish people, so Arieh Handler, from his teens, and for nigh on 80 years thereafter, was imbued with the mission of rescue, of survival. Both speaker and listener in May 1948 shared qualities of courage and loyalty to their people and its traditions.

Ben-Gurion, in a way the father of his people in their new State, a George Washington, remained the public face of Israel for decades. Arieh Handler, constantly active at the grass roots, in country after country, was engaged, without public acclaim, in a rare, selfless campaign of rescue of souls. Because of Ben-Gurion a State was born. Because of Arieh Handler, many people in peril survived.

The story of Ben-Gurion, so well-known, is told in numerous books, biographies, histories, films, but the story of Arieh Handler, modest, dedicated, but also heroic, has never been told. It is a story well worth telling.

Suddenly, in May 2008, the world's media burst into the life of this 93 year-old in his modest Jerusalem home. Questions were directed at him, a film made of his responses. His name, and round, smiling face, were reflected on television screens across the world, for Arieh Handler, Jewish patriot, was one of the few persons still alive, who had sat in that crowded room and listened to his friend announce the birth of the State.

Just as Arieh had ensured the survival of so many afflicted souls, from Germany to Ethiopia, from the Soviet Union to North Africa, he was himself, to his surprise, a unique survivor. This book, also modest, is an attempt to portray the many-sided personality and achievements of an immensely likeable, unassertive individual, the friend of Prime Ministers, but, more importantly, the instrument of hope and redemption for thousands of ordinary people.

Chapter 2

FACE TO FACE WITH A MASS MURDERER

Arieh's rescue work extended to helping young Jews leave Germany. From 1935 he travelled throughout Western Europe seeking visas for young boys and girls for their onward journey to Palestine, despite opposition from the British, then in control of that country. In those fearful days every Jewish man in Germany had a 'J' stamped in his passport, and every Jewish woman, 'Sarah'. In some miraculous way Arieh's passport remained unstamped

In 1938 when Germany took over Austria, he and his good friend Yosef Burg, both in Berlin, received desperate calls from Vienna for help to get the young people out, but, at that time, no Jew was allowed to travel to Austria. Yosef and Arieh knew the danger but felt they had to respond to the desperate call for help. They decided to take the risk. They went by plane, filled with German Army officers, but arrived unnoticed.

Arieh records what happened next.

"Our chaverim (colleagues) in Vienna seemed very frightened. We started our work to organise our friends into solid groups that would survive Nazi measures. Burg left and got back to Germany. When the time came for me to return to Berlin I decided to travel by train and to book a sleeper. I realised that, if caught, I would immediately be sent to a concentration camp but I had no alternative".

Arieh was deeply concerned for his friends in Austria and the saving of their lives. However, his experience on the train was something he had not bargained for. He recalls:

"During the long journey I left my compartment to go to the toilet along the corridor. As I did so, I froze in terror. In front of me was Adolf Eichmann. He knew me from Berlin and would realise who I was and that

I had travelled illegally to Vienna. I expected him to point at me and ask his official to seize me. It was certainly the most dangerous moment of my life. I kept walking, expecting any moment a heavy hand on my shoulders and a shout of "Jude". But nothing happened. Nobody shouted, nobody moved. For some reason Eichmann decided he had not seen me".

Some years later, Eichmann, who had fled to South America, was captured and put on trial in Israel for the murder of six million Jews. This evil man, it should he noted, was the only person to receive a sentence of capital punishment in Israel's sixty years of existence.

That experience was one Arieh never forgot. Somehow fate or something had cleared a path for him. Perhaps it was his own unshakeable belief in the importance of what he was doing that drove him on.

From the age of 15 he had been involved with Jewish youth. He travelled tirelessly from 1935, when he was but 20 years old, to save his fellow-Jews. The evil shadow of Hitler and the Nazi madness spread over Europe. Until 1938 Arieh journeyed, in search of visas, from Berlin to country after country, Denmark, Sweden, England, Belgium, France and Italy, in his rescue operation. In Denmark, Sweden and Holland, he was successful, less so in France and England. Every visa obtained represented a passport to life.

The thought may occur as to how he could undertake these travels from Berlin, with all the Nazi restrictions in force. Again Eichmann comes into the picture. He was in charge of the Jewish Department of the Gestapo, that hateful, brutal body, and yet it was that very organisation that allowed Arieh to travel backwards and forwards in and out of Germany. They may have had their own reasons, but again was some kindly spirit helping? Arieh recalls:

"When I returned to Germany after each journey I had to report to the Gestapo and provide eight copies of a statement detailing every person I had met and where I spent my time. When I left out details of my visit to Chief Rabbi Hertz in London, the Gestapo knew all about it".

How anyone else would have felt at constant contact with the Gestapo is not difficult to speculate. It would have been the last thing any Jew would have wanted. But clearly Arieh Handler, a shaliach (messenger) for life, cared little about his own when the future of thousands was at stake.

Yet how did this young man, still in his twenties, determined, courageous, ever-active, became involved in the fervent struggle to save his fellow Jews? Perhaps, this is a suitable time to look at where he had come from, his family, his background, his early years.

Chapter 3

"KNOW FROM WHERE YOU HAVE COME
AND WHITHER YOU ARE BOUND"

These words derive from a saying of an ancient rabbi. Arieh, steeped in Jewish knowledge, would be well acquainted with Akavya ben Mehalalel of old. When a person devotes a lifetime to the needs of others, it is instructive to enquire into the roots of such activity.

The tiny Jewish people, with its unique history covering over 4000 years, provides so many examples of leadership, activity and study, at different levels, that its story is a veritable summary of the annals of mankind.

As to leadership, it is worth noting that Field Marshal Montgomery, himself a celebrated military leader of the Second World War, once declared that the story of Moses represented the greatest example of leadership in history. Translating beliefs into action has always been a feature of Jewish experience. Examples abound in the Bible, King David, Zerubavel, the Maccabees.

Famous Rabbi Hillel commented: "If I am for myself only, what then am I?", a teaching that imbued Arieh Handler's conduct of his own life, though he could also provide, from personal experience, the names of others whose lives reflected that precept, from child rescuer Henrietta Szold to his hero David Ben-Gurion.

One saying of a famous Chassid in particular applies to Arieh. Rabbi Susya once stated "in the world to come I will not be asked, why were you not Moses but rather why were you not Susya". Thus, an individual must use, in active life, those qualities with which he or she has been blessed. Arieh Handler never attempted to be Moses, or even Susya, but always to be Arieh Handler, whether amidst the horrors of the concentration camps he visited after 1945 or with famous Prime Minister friends. He knew his limitations, but he acted at times beyond those limitations, which is what courage is all about.

Unlike some other faiths, Judaism not only places deeds above beliefs, but also study and learning as higher than, or at least equal to, prayer, especially study of the gold mine of religious literature, from the Torah to the Prophets, the Mishnah to the Talmud, Zohar and medieval luminaries to the Nachmans, Dov Baers and Schneur Zalmans among the host of 18th century sages.

That constant, irrepressible, Jewish impulse to learn and to study, produced in the 20th century, an amazing burst of Jewish creativity, not least in science, culminating in Albert Einstein, the greatest scientist of all.

Thus, Arieh Handler, in his much more modest world, could draw on numerous models of leadership, of action, and of study. In attempting to put one's finger on the origins, the impulses, behind a lifetime of service, it is not unreasonable to indicate inspiring examples within his own tradition. Yet, on a more mundane level, there may be some evidence from his family background that impelled this most modest of men to make his distinctive mark on Jewish history.

Arieh did not emerge from a famous family. There were not amongst his forebears, men and women of renown, but rather, typical of their time and place, parents and grandparents who strove to do their best for their families and provide solid examples of upright behaviour. Arieh's father was Ephraim Handler who married Helena Schönwetter. They had four children, Moritz, Julius, Arieh, and a sister Henny, a name to appear again in Arieh's life.

Poland was then the home of a vast number of Jews. Among them, in the western part, near to Germany, lived his grandmother and in the eastern part, Galicia, his grandfather Yehuda. Arieh bears the marks of both worlds, the enthusiasm and warmth of the latter, the organising ability of the former. In the last part of the 19th century and later, Jews from Poland moved, whenever possible, away from the poverty and pogroms of that land. Arieh's grandparents, part of that emigration, were no exception.

Thus his father and mother met and married in Poland, but, when

Arieh was born, it was not in that country. He first saw the light of day in Brno, Czechoslovakia on 27th May 1915. He explains that his father was at the time an officer in the Austrian army - Brno was part of the Austro-Hungarian empire - stationed in that town. His mother, "like a good Jewish wife", went where her husband was. Hence, Czechoslovakia has the privilege to add the name Handler to its roll of honour.

The family at first moved to Halberstadt but later soon settled in the prominent city of Magdeburg, about 144 kilometres from Berlin. It was a good place for the father, already developing his many-sided business. So there, ensconced in that famous town, were the parents, Arieh, his sister and two brothers.

They were not the first Jewish inhabitants. Jews had dwelt there as long ago as the 10th century, facing the subsequent usual undulating policies and practices of official protection and official persecution. There was even a Jewish academy for study, a yeshiva, in the town in the 15th century, but, as happened so often in the Christian world, in 1492 Jews were expelled, the cemetery destroyed, and the synagogue turned into a chapel. Those destroyers, calling themselves followers of Jesus, forgot his own words "I come for the lost sheep of Israel". They were indeed lost sheep and many of them moved eastwards to Russia, Poland, and the Baltic States. Arieh's background was thus not exceptional but typical.

Also typical was the revival of the community years later. By the 19th century there were several thousand Jews living in the town. The vast majority were 'Liberal' Jews, only about 10%, including Arieh's family, being Orthodox. Both streams of Judaism however co-operated with each other.

Early Zionism began mainly with Chovevei Zion (Lovers of Zion) a religious movement in the 1880s, enlarged greatly by the leadership of Theodor Herzl in the 1890s, developed by his successors in the first decades of the 20th century. Zionism, the return to the old-new Land, Herzl's phrase, was very much in the air. Pioneers, chalutzim, went to work in the neglected, and often swamp-ridden land, including Ben-Gurion in 1906, whilst one of the world's earliest environmental bodies, Keren Kayemet LeYisrael (Jewish National Fund) was established in 1902, covering the arid land with hundreds of millions of trees in the century that followed.

There being no Jewish school in town, young Orthodox Arieh found himself a student in the local monastery school. He later quipped that "for four years I studied Latin and for two years Greek". One wonders how much of it remains, recalling to mind that Shakespeare was said to have had "little Latin and less Greek". Arieh was no Shakespeare. What he was though was a youth imbued with the Zionist ideal, as was his fellow-citizen Arthur Ruppin, who was to play a notable role in developing the infrastructure of the future State, just as members of Arieh's family who likewise went off to work on the land in Palestine, Arieh often uses the words 'Eretz Yisrael' (Land of Israel) to describe pre-state Palestine.

But the monastery, Greek and Latin, was not enough for his educationally - minded parents. So off he was sent to the famous Jewish community of Frankfurt (original home of the Rothschilds), spending two years in a yeshiva, studying, studying, yet still, surprisingly, learning Latin and Greek one day a week at the highly regarded Lessing Gymnasium.

Thus, there came together the pursuit of knowledge, the heady influence of nascent Zionism, as well as examples of the chalutzim going off to till the ancient Judean soil. Study and activity came together. Leadership was to follow. The learned 15-year old was about to put his ideas and feelings into practice, whilst recalling the mounting problems of the country.

"I think my avid interest in politics and public life started when Germany suffered horrendous inflation. My father, who was very active in business and trade, had to go to the bank with a van on a Friday to collect money in sacks to pay his employees. My father ran three businesses, metal and scrap, picture framing and textiles, and was reasonably prosperous. But the economic situation of the country was disastrous. Unemployment was rampant".

Young, perceptive, Arieh realised then that despite all the efforts of the Social Democratic party, there was "a rising tide of national chauvinistic feeling of the German people". That tide swept on through the 1930s, fanned by the malevolent propaganda of the Nazis, finally exploding in the notorious Kristallnacht of 10 November 1938, when synagogues across Germany, including the main one in Magdeburg, were burned to the ground. Arieh and his family understood what was happening and what was likely to happen. It was this perception, not shared by some Jews who thought Nazism was just a passing phase, that led, in the 1930s to Arieh Handler the activist. Perhaps unconsciously, he felt it was a race against time.

Chapter 4

THE CHALLENGE OF THE THIRTIES

Winston Churchill once used the phrase 'the gathering storm' to describe the growing peril of that fateful decade before World War erupted in 1939. Whilst British and French politicians pursued appeasement, Nazi Germany rearmed and prepared for war. It was against this sombre background that Arieh developed those qualities of leadership that marked his future life.

His yeshiva years in Frankfurt were "how I got my Jewish Zionist education and learned to fulfil my duty as a Jew". It was there that enthusiastic Zionists surrounded him. It was there that he resolved to play a part not only in the dream of Eretz Yisrael but, more immediately, in facing the dangers gathering around the Jews of Germany, particularly the young people.

Even though but a 15-year old, observers noted his self-confidence, cheerfulness, energy, and capacity for friendship. Not surprising that he then formed Zionist youth groups, many of whose members later played a prominent role in religious kibbutzim in Israel.

He observed the wider picture of a Germany "economically and politically in a terrible state and that social calamity must lead to social unrest and a social explosion. We knew Germany would seek scapegoats in the world outside and in the Jews inside".

Back in Magdeburg, in 1931-32, Arieh completed his secular studies and matriculated. His father continued with his business but his fellow-Jews were becoming increasingly concerned. Nazism was on the march and, with it, the terrible virus of anti-Semitism. Jews were again becoming the scapegoat. If Jews were rich, they controlled everything. If Jews were poor, they were a burden. If they were on the Left, they were agents of Communist revolution. If they came from the East, as many did, with long beards and strange clothes, they were un-German.

The terrible, irrational disease of anti-Semitism spread among the general population, who found in it an excuse for their own troubles. The Nazis built on this resentment and fear, so that, by 1933, they had become the official government of the country, elected by popular vote. Thus did democracy lead to dictatorship. Thus began the nightmare that led to the destruction of one-third of the Jewish people, amidst the deaths of tens of millions across Europe.

Years later, members of his family pondered on what it was that catapulted Arieh into organisation after organisation, into positions of leadership, decade after decade, before the war, during the war, after the war, in Britain and in Israel. What was the motive force that drove him on, tirelessly. As he said, he felt a sense of duty as a Jew, a religious Jew. From that source he derived inspiration and perception.

Yet what noticeably emerged from his unique story is the total absence of personal ambition. He was not concerned about holding this or that office. His only concern was for the well-being of those for whose benefit the organisations were formed.

This absence of egoism, of desire for public fame and acclaim, made him such an attractive personality that he was welcomed universally by Jews, non-Jews, leading politicians, public figures. People instinctively saw that he was no threat to them. His only mission was the cause in hand. In the 1930s the causes were many, and this young man, just out of his teens, responded with the maturity and drive of a much older person.

Far removed from the 1930s, it is difficult now to conceive the problems of that era. His father had provided premises and a teacher for the new Talmud Torah school. Arieh developed from it a Brit Hanoar youth group which later became one of Arieh's great loves, Bnei Akiva. Unbelievably, he had to submit to the Gestapo his monthly programme, translating the Hebrew into German. Sometimes a Gestapo man actually attended the meetings. Among the wealth of documents he still possesses are copies of his reports and programmes.

Arieh resolved then that he had to rescue his people, especially the youth. He was determined to get Jewish boys and girls out of Germany. There was no future there. He established in Hamburg a Pioneer House training camp. He himself trained in agriculture and met leaders he admired greatly, Moshe Unna and heroic Enzio Sereni, both of whom had come from Palestine to train the youngsters. These men made an indelible impression on Arieh. He was filled with admiration for their enterprising spirit.

Another training camp near Frankfurt saw Arieh, as busy as ever, building another movement, Bachad, which, after the war, was to play a major role in his life. The word itself stood for religion, pioneering, union, all main elements in his life.

But there was yet another side to this young man. All very well to train pioneers, but to get them out of Germany was a problem. The answer was visas. By 1935 Arieh was in Berlin running Brit Hanoar and Bachad for the whole of Germany to which was added the office of joint director of Youth Aliyah, another great love of his through the decades ahead, inspired by a woman for whom he had the greatest admiration, Recha Freier.

In a way this dedicated lady, working alongside the better-known Henrietta Szold, set a daring example for the young activist. She told of her trips abroad to persuade the British Government to grant visas for young German Jews. Arieh recalls this inspiring person.

"All credit must be given to this remarkable woman. I remember vividly her visionary eyes. Without her there would not have been Youth Aliyah".

Another remarkable leader he met in Berlin was ill-fated Chaim Arlosoroff, head of the Political Department of the Jewish Agency, who, sadly, at 33, was to fall victim to a murderer's bullet. Arieh remembers him "as a man of vision, who had achieved so much in his young life, a tremendous loss". Arieh still shudders when he recalls the shock of the assassination.

Being a Jewish leader required courage. In trying to assess the qualities of Arieh, the impulse that took him through problem after problem, one notes that obviously he was physically tough, but that was not enough. As one surveys the range of his encounters, with Gestapo, with hate-filled Nazis around him, he needed also moral strength and courage. He needed these qualities too in travelling from town to town to encourage reluctant parents to send their children for training away from home.

Not all, understandably, agreed with him, but those that did, and their children, had reason to bless him. Many years later how often, in his 90s, did he exult in meeting them. How often did he turn to his neighbour, pointing to an elderly, bearded man with the word "he was one of my boys". And indeed they were. Whatever their age, to him, they remained his boys.

Without it ever entering his mind, there was about him a touch of that redemptive instinct, helping Jews to survive, for whatever reason, that typified the later actions of British Embassy official Captain Foley, of Schindler, of Wallenburg.

Another heart-stopping encounter. Travelling from Frankfurt to Munich, the train halted and SS officers entered his compartment. Near Munich was the infamous Dachau concentration camp where many Jews were held. Would they arrest him, interrogate him? Just being a Jew was enough of a crime. His heart stopped. But again some kindly, helpful spirit seemed to hover over him. The SS departed their way and Arieh his. He realised his luck but that he had to be constantly on his guard. The Nazis were no respecters of persons, especially Jewish persons.

In Berlin Arieh spent such little free time as he had studying in the Rabbinic Seminary. Another student, more full-time, was Yosef Burg. Here began a deep and lasting friendship, even unto the ninth decade of Burg's life. In those Berlin days, the two of them were constantly in touch, and throughout the years that followed, Burg figures so often in Arieh's stories and in his heart.

To relate all that Arieh did in the 1930s would require a separate volume to itself. He travelled to London, urged World Zionist leader, Dr. Chaim Weizmann to press the issues of Jewish immigration into Palestine and visas for Britain He saw Chief Rabbi Hertz who explained why he could not help, yet the Chief Rabbi sent 1000 copies of the Chumash

(Pentateuch) he had edited and notated, most of them ending up in the hands of the Gestapo who exulted in their destruction.

Arieh had great regard for the Marks and Spencer trio of families, the Marks, Sieffs and Sachers, all of whom were towers of strength and support before 1939 and in the State's subsequent struggle. He noted too the sympathetic understanding of the Zionist cause by C.P. Scott, famous editor of the Manchester Guardian but he was all the more disappointed when that journal, later known as the Guardian, departed from the policy and perception of its great editor.

Constantly travelling, he journeyed to Sweden where thousands of Jewish girls had been admitted. He wanted them to go to Palestine. He wanted them to maintain their Jewish roots but found little response from the assimilated Jewish leaders there. Some of the girls reached Palestine, some married non-Jews in Lapland to where they had been sent. A number, despairing, committed suicide.

Arieh attended the 1935 World Jewish Congress in Switzerland, and all subsequent Congresses. The big issue in 1935 was the possible partition of the Land, an issue that aroused strong feelings. Arieh was not concerned about partition, but with visas, with saving human beings. People, Jews, had to be saved. That was the vital issue. Arieh was a man of the people, for the people.

Looking back, years later, he expressed surprise that amidst all the turmoil of the time, he was able to see the situation so clearly.

"We thought the Western world did not understand Germany". He, and certainly Winston Churchill, did. He told parents: "Don't rely on the belief that things will get better". He may have been a political animal but he also had a prophet's touch.

Chapter 5

ARIEH TAKES A WIFE

At the end of 1938, working in London, he received a message from Dr. Burg that he should not return to Berlin as he would be arrested. Arieh stayed in Britain where he remained throughout the Second World War. From 1939 his efforts were directed from Woburn House, near Holborn, then the main Jewish communal centre in the capital. Both he and the building survived the worst the Germans could do. He talks with a certain pride of being on the rota for fire-watching. He and Rabbi Dr. Isidore Epstein, Principal of Jews College, used to watch out from the roof of the building for German incendiary bombs. There is no record that any landed on this Jewish centre, but fire-watchers had to stay up all night just in case. He worked there for Youth Aliyah, part of the Jewish Agency, and also for Bachad, for religious chalutzim.

Woburn House was also for years home of the Board of Deputies of British Jews, the body representing the Jews of the country. It had been founded in 1760 and, among its Presidents had been Sir Moses Montefiore, and later Professor Brodetsky, Lord Barnett Janner and his son Lord Greville Janner. It was the Janners who encouraged Arieh to become a Deputy and to play, at a later stage, a leading role at the Board, especially in relation to Israel.

The Jewish Agency, Youth Aliyah, Bachad, fire-watching, the war itself, were one thing, but soon a much more important event was to take place in the life of this 25-year old. Of course he was pleased Hapoel Hamizrachi in Jerusalem had asked him to take over the whole of Western European activities of the movement, but, more significant, personal matters were developing at the same time.

"Arieh adores Henny", stated Susan Sperber, Arieh's secretary, who knew the couple well. This adoration was not immediately obvious. What was obvious was Arieh's respect for his wife. When lost for a German or English word or when trying unsuccessfully to recall some important event in his life, he often turned to her for help, and always got it. Form the start of their relationship, Arieh had a dual feeling for Henny, love mixed with a healthy dose of respect.

This attitude was due apparently to Henny's striking personality. Tall, slim, tastefully dressed, she exuded a sense of confidence, a confidence bolstered by a discreet irony and distinctive sense of humour. Any bombastic statement by Arieh could easily be punctured by a gentle, ironic intervention accompanied by a slight smile. Arieh appeared for a considerable time to have been at a loss how to win this pretty, artistic, girl.

Henny was born in Berlin, the daughter of an enterprising businessman, Yitzhak Prilutzky, and a courageous, resourceful mother, Rivka. Yitzhak came to Berlin from Kiev, capital of the Ukraine, whilst Rivka was from Teplik, situated between Kiev and Odessa. They had left Russia in 1910 for Germany settling first in Königsberg. At the outbreak of the First World War, the couple moved to Berlin where Yitzhak established a modest tobacco business.

Rivka and Yitzhak had nine children, not then unusual among Orthodox Jews, five girls and four boys. Henny arrived after a sister and two brothers. She attended the ultra-Orthodox Adass School which today bears a memorial to the Jews killed by the Nazis.

Perceptive and lively, Henny saw and felt deeply the devastation wrought by the Nazis among the Jewish population.

"Every day you felt the squeeze on the Jews. When they lost one job and managed somehow to get another, that was soon lost. The Nazis constantly squeezed the Jews into corners to get rid of them. You could feel the terror, the uncertainty. Yet we young people somehow managed to adapt, as young people of all nations do. Somehow we managed to live and even to enjoy ourselves on occasions".

Henny was musically and artistically gifted. She played the violin particularly well. She later studied domestic science and was put in charge of the kitchen of the Rabbinic seminary.

"We fed the students and Arieh was one of them but I did not take any particular notice of him. There were other young men. Later he met me when I went for my violin lessons in another district where the Zionist pioneering training offices were situated. Somehow I still did not pay close attention. Arieh pretended that he was not interested in girls. He was too busy with his serious work of getting Jews out of Germany. We moved really in different circles".

In 1938 Henny's parents realised that the situation of the Jews was becoming so precarious that they had at all costs to leave Germany. But where were they to go? The borders of almost all countries were shut against Jews, but there were still some possibilities. With the help of Youth Aliyah, Henny's father managed to obtain three visas for England. One of them went to Henny, who recalled:

"It was very late in the summer and my parents were frantic to get us out. They feared that everyday we stayed our lives were in danger. They managed to get seven of their nine children out of Germany. They could not get visas for the last two or for themselves".

Henny's parents decided that her father should try to escape to France. He managed to get to Belgium from where he made his way to Paris. His wife, Rivka, stayed in Berlin with the remaining two children. On learning that Yitzhak had escaped, the Nazi authorities arrested Rivka and sent her to prison for six months. The children were looked after by friends.

An opportunity to save the two children suddenly arose and Rivka was determined to take it. Recha Freier, who, with Henrietta Szold, saved thousands of children through Youth Aliyah, was gathering the last group of German-Jewish children for sending to Palestine. Rivka handed over her two children to her. They arrived safely in Palestine, escaping first through Yugoslavia. Their later fate in the new country was tragic. One was killed in Israel's War of Independence in 1948. The other died from a sudden illness.

Rivka, after a terrifying ordeal, managed to cross the border into Belgium. She, too, made her way to Paris where she was reunited with Yitzhak. But they could not live together. She had false papers, whereas he used his own name. Henny, in London, kept in contact with her mother through the Red Cross. Yitzhak planned to escape to Switzerland but in

1942 was caught in a round-up in Paris and taken to Auschwitz where he died.

Rivka kept going by taking on menial jobs, sewing and looking after children. The Nazis never discovered her true identity and she survived. After the liberation in 1945 she found a place on the first boat that went to Palestine. The man who arranged her passage was Arieh.

Henny came to London in 1939. On her visa she was described as a domestic servant. Coming from such an Orthodox family she naturally found her friends in Bachad, religious pioneering circles. It was then that she met Arieh again. She quickly realised that he was seriously interested in her, but he was shy, apparently worried that he might be rebuffed. This was not the confident Arieh known to his male friends.

"Arieh" said Henny, "played a funny trick". Instead of approaching her directly, he invited her to his office saying that he wanted to talk about her younger sister, Golda, then at a Bachad training centre in East Lothian, Scotland. He was concerned, he said, about the young girl's welfare, though Henny realised the real reason for the meeting.

So their friendship began. Arieh and other members of Bachad invited Henny to give music lessons to young members and teach songs with rousing choruses once a week. "I made Arieh sing", she recalled with relish. Arieh was hesitant, apparently doubting his singing progress, but, encouraged by Henny, he appeared once or twice a week at the sessions. He was no doubt relieved to learn that no record remains of his performances.

It became obvious to Henny that Arieh wanted to marry her. They were meeting regularly and finding many things in common. Arieh was still uncertain whether Henny would accept him, but finally, in the midst of the Blitz in London, Arieh proposed and was accepted. In late December 1940 they were married in Gwrych Castle in Wales. It was a true Bachad wedding.

The Castle was a Bachad training centre and 200 German-Jewish children lived there, preparing for agricultural work in Palestine. They were the guests of the wedding, bride and groom surrounded by a host of smiling youngsters, his "boys and girls". The ceremony was conducted by

Rabbi Issar Yehuda Unterman, later Ashkenazi Chief Rabbi of Israel. Henny recalled:

"The Castle was bare and cold. In fact it was freezing when the wedding took place. There was very little food, but nobody cared about such small things, once the wedding started. We had to wait. Arieh was attending a conference of Bachad that day and was late for the wedding".

From her very first day of marriage Henny had come to know what to expect of her husband. Arieh being late or not even being present at important family occasions because of having to attend conferences and meetings was a fact Henny learned to accept. Arieh was not around when their second child, Gaby, was born in 1946. He had travelled to Palestine on what he believed was a vital party mission, staying away for over 4 months. He returned after the birth, bringing with him a box of chocolates! He was also prone to send a message to Henny, "I am bringing 30 people from the movement to the house".

In 1947 Henny went to Palestine with the two children, Danny having been born in 1944, where she met the surviving members of her family. Arieh soon joined join her and they were involved in the War of Independence.

Henny once said,

"Arieh resides in England but lives in Israel. Arieh is totally absorbed in Israeli life. This absorption in Eretz Yisrael started when he was very, very young, as young as 14. There are very few people in the world who care so much for Israel. He is restless every minute in the day to know what is happening in Israel. It is his life. Nothing comes before Israel".

Henny loyally supported him in all he did throughout their long lives together. The war prevented Arieh from travelling abroad, but travel he did, all over Britain in the cause of the youngsters he had helped to rescue.

Chapter 6

WARTIME BRITAIN 1940-1945

Arieh, the non-stop traveller, now had to confine his activities to Britain. In 1938 he had travelled three times to Palestine, also to Norway in pursuit of visas. He was ever in pursuit of visas to enable escape from Germany. Where visas were obtained, Arieh could arrange for people to leave Germany, but he was immensely frustrated by those countries that did not realise the tragic circumstances of Jews in Germany and were sparing in the grant of visas.

Before the war erupted in September 1939, he had managed to get both his parents and a brother to leave for Palestine. He threw himself into his efforts in London which he also regarded as a form of rescue work. This involved helping to train and settle all those youngsters, many of whom had come on what became known as Kindertransport, several thousand young people saved from the Nazis. He faced the challenge with his usual energy, now buoyed up by the support of his wife.

This effort, through Bachad, took two forms, first the development of training centres and, secondly, obtaining the organised support of prominent British Jews. The former resulted in centres being set up where the young people could live, train and learn about their Jewish traditions. Such centres included Gwrych Castle in Wales, the scene of his joyous wedding, Whittingehame, a country seat belonging to Lord Balfour but given for use during the war. Other centres were as far afield as East Lothian in Scotland, St. Asaph in Wales, and farms in Devonshire. He was particularly moved by the offer by Quakers (of Cadbury fame) who provided a training centre in Bromsgrove, near Birmingham, known as Avonscroft College. It provided a home for 80 boys and girls. Henny, faithful, industrious wife, became the supervisor and Matron of all kitchen and domestic arrangements there.

Of course, that kept the newly-married couple apart since Arieh operated from London. In order to be together, Arieh spent every weekend in Avonscroft. He recalled how he sometimes took with him Chaim (then known as Vivian) Herzog, at the time an officer in the British Army and subsequently a President of the State of Israel.

Arieh was particularly intrigued by Rabbi Dr. Louis Jacobs, later a famed scholar, but then a rabbinical student. Louis, whose future wife trained in Avonscroft, was deeply concerned whether there was a sufficient degree of kashrut observed in the camp.

Another centre was Merkaz Limmud in Manchester where boys and girls could train and study together. Among the teachers were Rabbi Sperber and Hans Heinemann, author of Torah and Social Order, and later a distinguished Professor of Judaism at the Hebrew University.

As the war progressed many young men were called to the British forces. Farmers needed help. This provided an opportunity for some of Arieh's youngsters to work on farms, even to live in farmhouses, often in small remote places. Arieh travelled the length and breadth of the country visiting the centres and the young people.

At the same time, he looked around for wider support from among British Jews. There was the Central British Fund (CBF) dedicated to work for refugees. There was, in Bloomsbury House, a centre where volunteers came to feed and help the youngsters. These volunteers, Arieh recalled, were fine, well-meaning people, but they did not understand fully the longer term needs of the youngsters. So Arieh decided to form a new organisation, Bachad.

To this end he enlisted the support of prominent British Jews who were to play an important role in his future work. He laid the foundation of friendships that endured. Those qualities of organisational ability, devotion to the cause, Jewish loyalty, and capacity for friendship, stood him in good stead then and in later years.

In 1939 he was instrumental in organising a Jewish Agricultural Committee to support Bachad and the work it was doing. Arieh became Honorary Secretary. A financial expert Desmond Hirshfield (later a peer)

Arieh in Bar Kochba uniform - Magdeburg 1927

Castle couple: Arieh Handler and his wife, Henny, surrounded by Gwrych residents on their wedding day in December 1940

At Kibbutz Tirat Tzvi with Moshe Shapira

Arieh, Mark Persoff, Oscar Philip, Ben-Zion Margulies and Alex Margulies

A Bachad Fellowship meeting at the Bachad Fellowship Farm, Thaxted

R to L. Arieh with Mrs. Rebecca Sieff during the establishment of Kibbutz Lavi

Arieh with Dr. Tibor Rosenbaum

Lady Wingate and Moshe Kol at the founding of Yemin Orde Children's Village (Arieh with hat)

*Arieh and
Dr. Yosef Burg*

With Eli Reichmann of Tangier Jewish community arriving in Madrid

With Prime Minister Levi Eshkol (centre) and Dr. Yosef Burg

With Sephardi Haham, Dr. Abraham Gaon and Israel Consul Sivan

With Moshe Unna and Moshe Shapira

Golda Meir, Lord Samuel Fisher, Dr. Levenberg and Arieh with Prime Minister Harold Wilson

*Arieh and good friend
Harold Wilson*

With Chief Rabbi Dr. Israel Brodie

With Director of Yavneh Yeshiva Rav Goldwicht

For Soviet Jews. With Prime Minister Margaret Thatcher, Lord Greville Janner, Edgar Bronfmann, Isi Liebler, Eliahu Dobkin, Arieh Dulchin and others

With King Hussein of Jordan and Jewish Chronicle Chairman

With Israel's President Chaim Herzog greeting Arieh's wife Henny

With Prime Minister Margaret Thatcher

*With Chaim Herzog, Elieser Scheffer, Solly Sachs, Chief Rabbi Mordechai Eliyahu,
and Government Ministers Zvulun Hammer and Yitzhak Levi*

Rally for Soviet Jews with Chief Rabbi Lord Immanuel Jakobovits and Avital Sharansky

With Natan Sharansky

With Refusenik Ida Nudal

*Presentation to Arieh
by Aubrey Rose*

With Chief Rabbi Lau

With lifelong friend Dr. Yosef Burg

At The Institute for the Blind, Israel, with Chayim Rashalbach

At Re'ut Foundation in Israel with Miriam Frankel

With Chief Rabbi Lord Immanuel Jakobovits

With Prime Minister Tony Blair

With Chief Rabbi Lord Jonathan Sacks and Israel Ambassador Tzvi Shtauber

Some sidelights on Arieh

מ נ ה ל ת ה ע ם

תל-אביב , ד ' אייר תש"ח
13 . 5 .1948

א. נ. ,

הננו מתכבדים לשלום לך בזה הזמנה

ל מ ו ש ב

ה כ ר ז ת ה ע צ מ א ו ת

שיתקיים ביום ו', ה' באייר תש"ח
(14.5.1948) בשעת 4 אחה"צ באולם
המוזיאון (שדרות רוטשילד 16).

אנו מבקשים לסגור בסוד את תוכן
ההזמנה ואת מועד כינוס המועצה.

המוזמנים מתבקשים לבוא לאולם
בשעה 3.30.

בכבוד רב

ת ס ו כ י ר ו ת

ההזמנה היא אישית   -   תלבסת; בגדי חג בהים

Invitation to attend Declaration of Israel's Independence on 14 May 1948

68

The Peoples' Administration [Minhelet Ha'Am]

Tel Aviv, 4th of Iyar 5708
13.5.1948

Dear Sir,

We are honoured to send you this invitation

To the Session of
The Declaration of Independence

Which will take place on
Friday, 5th of Iyar (14.5.1948)
at 4 o'clock in the afternoon in the hall of
the Museum (16 Rothschild Boulevard).

We ask that you keep the contents of the
invitation and the time of
the assembly of the Council secret.

Invitees are requested to come to the hall
at 3.30.

Most sincerely,
The Secretariat

This invitation is personal - Dress: dark festive clothes.

English Translation

PRIDE • CELEBRATION • GOLDEN JUBILEE • ACHIEVEMENT

COMMEMORATIVE CERTIFICATE

Henny & Arieh Handler

has been inscribed in the 50th Anniversary Scroll
to celebrate Israel's Golden Jubilee

50 years of achievement, 50 years of growth
50 years of pride, 50 years of life

1948	1998
תש"ח	תשנ"ח

וקדשתם את שנת שנת החמשים שנה וקראתם דרור בארץ לכל ישביה (ויקרא כה:י)

And you shall hallow the fiftieth year and proclaim liberty throughout the
Land of Israel to all its inhabitants (Leviticus XXV.10)

WOMEN'S
UJIA

ANNIVERSARY
SCROLL

CHIEVEMENT • UNITY • INDEPENNDENCE • HERITAGE • MILESTONE • LIBERTY

UJIA Certificate given to Henny and Arieh Handler in 1998

בס"ד

This certificate is presented to

Arieh Handler

on the occasion of the sixty-fifth anniversary of
Bnei Akiva of Great Britain and Ireland

Your vision has been a real source of inspiration
to chaverim of Bnei Akiva past and present

יהי חסדך ה' עלינו כאשר יחלנו לך

תעודה זו מוגשת לאריה הנדלר בעבור שנות עבודתו למען בני עקיבא

March 2004   Nisan 5764

Bnei Akiva Certificate presented to Arieh in March 2004

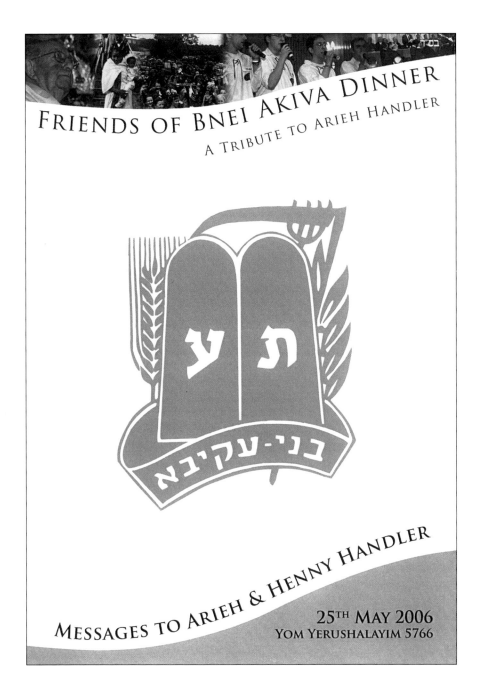

Bnei Akiva Tribute to Arieh and Henny in May 2006

EYE WITNESS

1948: THE DECLARATION OF INDEPENDENCE ARIEH HANDLER

David Ben Gurion (*left*) signs the declaration in Tel Aviv on May 14, 1948, witnessed by Foreign Minister Moshe Sharett (*right*)

I watched as the state was born

THE WRITER

● Arieh Handler, 92, is the last man still alive who was present when the declaration that created the state of Israel was signed by David Ben-Gurion

TO TELL the truth, I didn't think I would still be here to see Israel at 60 years old. But I am still very active, and active people live longer. I was one of the witnesses in that room where David Ben-Gurion signed the declaration. That was the night the Egyptians bombed Tel Aviv and the time when Glubb Pasha led the Arab armies against us. He was stopped at a place where today stands Tel Aviv University, where my son is a professor. On that night, we were dancing in the streets we were so happy. You cannot imagine what the declaration of the state meant to us. Many people in America

particularly, President Truman among them, told Ben-Gurion to wait a bit. But he ignored them and made the declaration. If he had waited, I am sure the state would never have been established. The only nation that wanted him to go ahead, strangely enough, was Russia. The Russians were hoping that with so many Labour people in power, it would be good for the Soviets.

The atmosphere in the small room was full of anticipation. Many people from Jerusalem who were supposed to sign couldn't get there because the Arabs had it surrounded, so they signed later. We were invited at 3pm and the signing started at 4pm. Ben-Gurion and on or

two other people spoke, but the speeches were short.

Amazingly, for a Jewish event it finished on time at 5.30, because it was Friday and Shabbat The whole thing was run by Ben-Gurion. He wanted all the political parties to sign the declaration and then we had a very big *l'chaim*. I was a

We knew then that we were witnessing history

young man, then only 32, but we knew that we were witnessing history, particularly after everything that the Jewish people had been through during the war.

It was undoubtedly the greatest day of my life.

Arieh's comment in 2008 on the Ceremony of Independence

73

'I was at Israel's founding'

When the State of Israel was declared on 14 May 1948, some 200 dignitaries were invited to the ceremony, held at the Museum of Art in Tel Aviv. Of those present, only one, Arieh Handler, now 93, is known to still be alive. Here he recounts his personal recollections of that historic day.

Mr Handler was told to keep his invitation a secret

I lived in a place not far from Israel's first prime minister, David Ben-Gurion, and I got the invitation from someone who came on a motorbike.

He handed it to me and did not say another word. I asked him what it was, and he said he was not allowed to tell me.

At the same time I got a telephone call, from one of Ben-Gurion's staff, and they asked me not to tell anybody that I had got this invitation.

But of course in a way that was rubbish because a few hours later everybody knew about it.

I still have the original invitation. It reads: 'From the Administration of the Nation, Tel Aviv, 13 May 1948. We are honoured to send to you this invitation to the session of the declaration of independence. It will take place on Friday, 14 May 1948, at four o'clock in the afternoon in Museum Hall, 16 Rothschild Boulevard.

'We request that you keep the content of this invitation and the date of the convention of the council a secret. Invited guests are requested to come to the hall at three-thirty. Sincerely, the secretariat. The invitation is personal. Dress: Dark, smart.'

I had this feeling in me that this was a historic moment, not just for the Jews but for the world

I got the invitation just 24 hours before the meeting took place. At that time, just one day before, it was still not clear whether Ben-Gurion would declare the state.

I was a member of the Zionist General Council [the governing body of the Jewish people in Palestine], and at that time there were telegrams coming from New York, from US President Harry S Truman and from Jewish friends of Truman, who pleaded with us not to declare the state, because they feared it would become a Soviet satellite, because the Russians supported it.

Ben-Gurion was in a difficult position but he told a small circle of us: "I'm not a communist and I would like to get the support of the Americans, but if I don't declare the state now, it will never happen". I agreed with him.

'Tremendous excitement'

I will never forget it. We were called to the meeting, it started at four o'clock, the state was declared, and it finished on the dot

at five-thirty - such punctuality never normally happens at a Jewish function!

I had this feeling in me that this was a historic moment, not just for the Jews but for the world.

When I left the meeting to go back to my family, Egyptian planes were already bombing Tel Aviv, and Glubb Pasha [the British commander of the army of Transjordan] was leading an Arab army - they were stopped by the Haganah [Jewish defence force] not far from where I lived.

Despite all these troubles, there was tremendous excitement. People were dancing in the streets, day and night, even as the planes were bombing, because they felt that the country would be a kind of solution for the Jewish problem.

In some respects I would not have believed that the state would develop so strongly - our universities, schools, businesses - they are tremendous! Things turned out better than I would have believed.

At the same time I am worried about one thing: if Jews and Arabs - who are good people - in this country will not make an effort to work and to live together then it will be bad for all of them.

Better leadership

I believe that the leadership of the country in the early years of the state was stronger and better than it is today.

At that time the leaders were people like Ben-Gurion, [prime ministers] Moshe Sharett, Golda Meir, Levi Eshkol - these were party people but they were people who had tremendous strength and power - I wish we had now the kind of leadership we had then.

It was difficult back then - we did not have enough money, we did not

Ben-Gurion was under pressure from some quarters to delay the declaration.

have enough weapons, but the people who were running the country knew what they were doing.

They wanted to find a way to integrate the Arab people into this new country, and I would say if this line would have been followed we would have had less problems today in the Middle East.

I would say many things - not only in the Jewish world, but in the world on the whole - would have been different if Ben-Gurion had not declared this state.

This is really why until today, my greatest day in life remains - and I am not a youngster any more - this simple meeting in the museum in Tel Aviv.

Interview by Raffi Berg

Arieh's interview with the BBC in May 2008

became Honorary Treasurer. The Committee was chaired by Rebecca Sieff, wife of Israel Sieff. Other members included Elaine Laski, wife of Neville, and of the Marks family. Professor Norman Bentwich, who had been Attorney General in the 1920s under the British Mandate in Palestine, was also involved.

Other supporters who gave of their time and money included the brothers Benzion and Alexander Margulies, Oscar Philip, Abba Bornstein, Mark Persoff, Desmond Hirschfield as well as Professor Brodetsky. Arieh had created links which were to bear fruit in later years. Thus, alongside the daily volunteers who helped with immediate needs, this group of influential people supported Arieh in the establishment of training centres for the young people in their long-term needs.

He recalls other episodes on the outbreak of war. He may not have been aware that, in the First World War, anyone with a German-sounding name risked attacks to person and property. A mere 20 years after that encounter, concern about those coming from Germany remained. Everyone with a German passport had to report to the police. This did not apply to Henny who was stateless. The authorities were concerned that, among those with such passports, the Germans may have placed spies and were therefore very much on their guard.

Arieh, whose German passport showed his name, Leon – though Arieh was how he was known to everybody – trooped along to St. John's Wood police station in London with a suitcase in each hand, anticipating that he might be interned. Many were so held for a time in the Isle of Man. But the good fairy who seemed to accompany him waved her magic wand again. Arieh was told by the Police Superintendent to go home. A possible explanation is that someone had informed the Home Office that Arieh could be of more use to the authorities outside than inside. And indeed, that became the case as the police asked for his advice as to the bona fides of individuals.

Any attempt to describe the work of this ever-active man whilst Britain was at war would result in a mass of details and documents, perhaps to be included in some fuller account of his life. Obviously, while deepening his links with members of Jewish community in Britain, he watched anxiously while the battle in North Africa, close to Palestine, flowed to and fro. However, he remained in touch with his family in the Yishuv, the description of the Jewish community in Palestine.

Behind all his efforts he felt that the boys and girls were not only training, but would later play an important part in any future Jewish state. And that in fact is what happened. Thousands of those whom Arieh had rescued and trained later became in his own words "builders of Israel".

Chapter 7

TOWARDS THE STATE 1945 - 1948

On 8th May 1945 the streets of London were filled with cheering, excited crowds. The Germans had surrendered unconditionally. The war in Europe was over. Gone were the black-out, and the Blitz, whilst the terrifying V1 and V2 missiles and rockets would fall from the sky no more. Even fire-watching was at an end. There was universal joy in London, an excitement and a sense of relief that surrounded Arieh.

He did not rejoice in the same way. This engaging, industrious 30-year old with a lovely, supportive wife, and one young son Danny (Gaby was born in 1946), though relieved at the ending of hostilities, reflected on the cost and on the tragedy that had befallen his people.

The extent of the horror, in May 1945, was not yet fully realised, but Arieh reflected on the failure of the democracies to understand before 1939 the extent of the dangers Jews were facing. He had fought and fought for visas for years, but the West, including the United States, had largely spurned his rescue efforts. For that was what the 1930s meant to him, a decade of rescue. That theme was to become even more pronounced in the years ahead.

He had seen the reticence of some of the long-established wealthier Jews in Britain to help in his mission. During the war he had observed the refusal to permit the founding of a Jewish Army. It was only after much agitation that a Jewish Brigade was formed, a unit that fought bravely alongside the Allies in Italy. Who had a greater reason to fight the Nazis! He realised, especially, that his people were but pawns in the larger political game, and that "only we ourselves will be able to fight for Eretz Israel and defend it".

The ensuing three years, from May 1945 to May 1948, were years of enormous challenge to the Jewish people throughout the world, to the leaders in the Yishuv especially, and to the man sitting in Woburn House, determined to play his part, whatever that might he, in Jewish redemption.

He was still doing all he could for Bnei Akiva, Bachad, and the religious Labour group, Hapoel Hamizrachi, still travelling, speaking, and writing. Arieh became a highly regarded editor over the years of journals such as Chayenu and The Jewish Review. But these years which saw him and his family move to Palestine in 1947 were dominated by two issues, the movement towards statehood, and the urgent need to help and rescue those survivors who still suffered and lay destitute and afflicted, physically and mentally, in those same camps, then referred to as Displaced Persons (DPs).

Many volumes have been written about the storms and stresses that led up to the birth of the State. The sole role of Britain in the land was to facilitate the creation of a "Jewish National Home" as stated in the 1917 Balfour Declaration. That role was confirmed by the League of Nations Mandate in 1923. Thus Palestine was never part of the British Empire. Britain was in Palestine as a trustee with a specific objective.

To a limited extent Britain tried to carry out this role, but always constricted by its own conception of Empire and by increasing concern at Arab riots in 1929 and 1936, as well as regard for the size and resources, actual and potential, of Arab lands.

In 1923 the borders of original Palestine were much reduced by the creation of the artificial state of Transjordan, later termed Jordan, where British influence reigned. In Palestine however there developed a growing Jewish population, approaching 600,000 by 1939, bolstered by many immigrants, from Germany especially. The latter, like Arieh himself, had certain organisational and professional abilities which enhanced the character of the Yishuv, the community led by a National Council known as Va'ad Leumi.

In the summer of 1945 a General Election in Britain resulted in the victory of the Labour Party. Churchill the great war hero, admirer and supporter of the Jewish people, as Sir Martin Gilbert illustrates in his book on the subject, stated, "I have been dismissed by the British people". In came Labour and a new Foreign Secretary, Ernest Bevin, a trade union organiser, on whom Jewish hopes rested. This was not unreasonable as, in the General Election, Labour had strongly supported the Zionist cause.

But a new Haman now arose. Bevin, with Cabinet support, and no doubt influential voices in the British Foreign Office, completely reversed the former Labour policy. They backed the White Paper issued in 1939 by Chamberlain's Conservative government which severely restricted Jewish immigration to Palestine. That White Paper – the colour is appropriate – was one aspect of the appeasement mentality of Prime Minister Chamberlain, typified by the infamous 1938 Munich Agreement with Germany.

It is interesting that pugnacious Ben-Gurion commented, "We shall fight the White Paper as if there were no war, and we shall fight the war as if there were no White Paper".

The new Government had however to bear in mind that the 1937 Peel Commission in London had recommended the partition of Palestine into two states, one Jewish, the other Arab.

Bevin was also embarrassed, though one finds it difficult to envisage that corpulent figure being embarrassed by anything, by a recommendation in 1947 of a Joint Anglo-American Commission that 100,000 Jewish refugees be allowed to enter Palestine.

America had become the dominant power in the political world. Under the Presidency of Franklin Roosevelt from 1933 to 1944 she had grown from a depressed nation to one of great economic power and self-confidence. She could bring influence to bear. President Truman backed the Commission's proposal. Bevin refused to accept it. Behind these political moves, this chess game of power politics, lay the continuing tragedy of the homeless Jewish remnants in Europe, many seeking Palestine as their ultimate goal, as well as the increasing peril of Jews in Arab lands. Ships with Jewish survivors on them were boarded. In the Struma 700 lives were lost. The story of the Exodus is well documented. Jews were diverted to Cyprus. Some languished for four years in Mauritius.

This was the background to the fierce debate in 1946 and 1947 within the Jewish world on the subject of partition. It is understandable that on this issue there was deep division, between parties and within parties, even between old colleagues and friends. Eretz Israel was being reduced, stage by stage. This revolted the Revisionists led by Jabotinsky and a later Prime Minister, Menachem Begin. It was of course from the extreme Right that violence came, the murder of Lord Moyne, the blowing up of a wing of the King David Hotel, the work of the Irgun. Weitzmann and Arieh condemned the violence.

Under the heading"Force is not enough", Arieh wrote,

"We can only condemn those who commit acts of violence. Terrorism by any Jews will become a boomerang hitting back at all Jews".

At the same time he had no such reservations for the British press as to their total lack of sympathy for the Displaced Persons. Arieh did not mince his words. He felt deeply for his people.

After attending the World Jewish Congress in 1946 in Basle, scene of the first Congress in 1897, Arieh again attacked the acts of violence.

But the mood of that Congress was opposed to the conciliatory views of aged Dr. Chaim Weitzmann who relied heavily on the good faith of Britain. Congress refused to attend any further suggested Conference in London. Weitzmann ceased to be President of the Congress though later, for a short while, he was President of the new State of Israel. It was Arieh's group, Hapoel Hamizrachi, that contributed to Weitzmann's defeat. It was Britain now that stood between the DPs in the camps,"the remnants", and their new life in Palestine. It was Britain that had now abandoned its obligation under the Balfour Declaration and the Mandate.

How ironic was Britain's attitude in that, in 1947, when it opposed the legitimate demands of the Jewish people, not part of the Empire and Commonwealth, as Weitzmann had once suggested, but had yet given independence to both India and Pakistan, then very much part of the Empire.

There were painful divisions on partition in the World Zionist movement. The issue was simple. Would the movement accept an independent state in a small part of the land? Ben-Gurion and Arieh and others felt this should be accepted, however reluctantly. At least those in Europe, waiting in despair, would have a homeland. In the Land, the

Revisionists would back no compromise. Some General Zionists, Weitzman, Brodetsky, Dr. Stephen Wise were in favour, others like Rabbi Abba Hillel Silver were opposed. On the Left, the young men, Arieh, his friend Yosef Burg, Moshe Shapira, backed Ben-Gurion. They were of the Labour Movement, the Histadrut, and worked for a social democratic state, even if only in part of Eretz Israel.

1947 became the crucial year. Bevin and his advisers threw up their hands in despair. Their policy was in ruins. The withdrawal of the British and the end of the Mandate was declared. Later, on 29th November 1947 the United Nations voted in favour of the creation of the new Jewish State.

Early in 1947 a meeting of the Zionist General Council took place in Tel Aviv, even as Arabs were attacking areas around Jerusalem. That meeting confirmed Ben-Gurion's view as to statehood. But also at that meeting the grounds for the State were prepared. The Haganah Defence Force was instructed as to its operations. The school system, health, sanitation, immigration, all were being prepared ahead of statehood. Arieh wryly noted, "even driving licences were made available. Yes, all was prepared slowly but thoroughly for the great day".

On Friday morning, May 14, 1948 a motor cyclist arrived at Arieh's home in Tel Aviv, bringing an invitation to "Chaver Handler" from the National Council of the Yishuv inviting him to attend the proclamation of the State of Israel. Despite pressure from individuals and governments to delay any such announcement, Ben-Gurion went ahead. The State was launched that afternoon. There was ecstatic dancing in the streets. Arieh had a modest role that day. Ben-Gurion the secularist, had brought Rabbi Fishman, later known as Maimon, and a second rabbi from encircled Jerusalem by light plane. He wanted them to be beside him as he made his declaration. After the ceremony Ben-Gurion asked Arieh to look after the two Rabbis and get them to their hotel before the sunset of the Sabbath on that historic Friday afternoon. Arieh complied willingly. He still has the invitation and produced it proudly to the world's media when they descended on him en masse in May 2008, 60 years later.

Chapter 8

THE CAMPS

Arieh was certainly a political animal, but much more. From his personal experiences and the teachings of his religion he knew he had to be of help to others"If I am for myself only, what then am I?". While his political work continued, behind it all were the urgent needs of his people in Israel, and especially in the camps. Physical aid was not enough. The survivors needed moral and spiritual help to overcome the nightmares they had endured

What had happened had never occurred before. That a country, regarded as civilised, had decided to treat fellow human beings, Jews, blacks, gypsies, homosexuals, the aged and disabled, as sub-human and exterminate them was unique in human history.

The Germans, hypnotised and mesmerised by intense racist propaganda, had themselves sunk to the sub-human lowest depths. Churchill described Hitler as "the embodiment of many forms of soul-destroying evil".

All Arieh's instincts impelled him to help personally and organise others to assist. To this end, one day, to the quiet amusement of Henny, he even appeared in a British Army uniform!

Immediately the Second World War ended, Arieh accompanied Chief Rabbi Hertz on a visit to the former Nazi death camps where millions of Jews had met their deaths. Yaacov Herzog, the brilliant younger son of Chief Rabbi Herzog of Palestine, joined Dr. Hertz and Arieh. Yaacov, who had a Semicha (rabbinical ordination) was later chosen to succeed Rabbi Dr. Israel Brodie as Chief Rabbi, but developed a fatal illness and died tragically young.

"We went from camp to camp and tried to bring hope to the tragic inmates", Arieh recalls. "This was before the great rescue operations.

People speak of the physical side of those victims, the men and women looking like skeletons and some dying from the effects of hunger and disease. But this is a simple approach. What was to be admitted is that not all the survivors were necessarily of the highest calibre morally." Arieh, the realist, understood the urge just to survive.

"The rescue work was carried out by Zionists of both the Right and Left. There was full cooperation. A bright young Londoner, Stanley Abramovich, a member of Bachad, even helped us to establish a yeshiva. He was one of the young men, almost a boy, whom I persuaded at the end of the war to join in our work and go to the DP camps. By chance he went to the American zone. He worked so exceptionally well in rehabilitating survivors that he was invited to become an official of the great American Joint Distribution Committee. After work in African countries and in Iran he became head of the Joint's Yeshiva Department in Jerusalem.

"My job was to persuade people to take over responsibility in the rescue work and become active in Jewish life. We urgently needed leaders but they had to be of the right quality and had to be both idealistic and capable. These two qualities, do not, alas, always go together.

"We sent 30 young men to the camps. This was done in cooperation with the Central British Fund. We all appreciated Professor Bentwich's leadership. I never heard any complaints about him, only praise. He was, indeed, a fine man and a fine Jew. We also persuaded the Jewish communal leaders to get the British Government to send officials to help in the camps. Several relief units were sent from Britain.

"I believe our effort from Britain has been underestimated. It was a vital part of the tremendous rehabilitation operation in the camps. To work among the young survivors and educate them for a new life was a marvellous task. There were many fine results. One of those who emerged from the camps was Shalom Markovitch who became one of the founders of Kibbutz Lavi, one of the finest kibbutzim in Israel and an inspiration for religious youth".

Arieh later wrote:

"My job was to bring up a generation of religious leaders, some of whom continue to work with us today. I regard this period, when I worked together with great personalities, as one of the most productive of my life. It was vital to rescue many of those in the camps not only physically but spiritually. Some of them might have become criminals, having lost all trust in society and humanity. They might have become enemies of society".

Rejecting firmly some of the "simplistic" descriptions of the camps and of the survivors and of those trained to help them, Arieh asked a rhetorical question: "Do you think we could simply take anyone to the boats to join the Exodus 47 in Marseilles as it prepared to set out with thousands of survivors for Eretz Israel? No, they had to be given a very good Zionist and Jewish education. We sent from this country, Britain, our boys and girls to the boats. They went with the survivors, wherever they were sent by the British after being caught by the British navy. Some went to Cyprus, some were returned to Germany on the Exodus when the ship was sent back by Ernest Bevin to Hamburg.

"Some of the survivors had gone through such terrible experiences that they felt like animals, crushed and dehumanised. There were others who went to Frankfurt and Munich and built up businesses. The vast majority were just relieved to be alive and looking with a mixture of hope, foreboding and pain for the new life that awaited them".

Even at the risk of offending a number of people, Arieh insisted that it was wrong to refer to the conditions in the camps with sentimental eyes, where everyone who survived was presented as a hero. A minority did present problems, and this had to be admitted.

"I worked as a Zionist official, as a religious man of our movement and as an educationist in the camps", Arieh said. "We had to start schools and kindergartens. The British military authorities did not allow us to take the survivors to Eretz Israel. But we could establish Jewish institutions in Europe. This we did quickly because we realised – and the British did not -- that they would prove crucial in fulfilling our aim to make these survivors citizens of the Jewish State that was being born.

"We had outstanding young people working for us. One such person was Benno Penner, from Glasgow. He was a source of inspiration to the survivors sent to Cyprus. When Golda Meir was sent by Ben-Gurion to

Cyprus to visit the survivors the man who was in charge was Benno.

"I take tremendous pride in these religious boys who helped to create ideals for a new life for the survivors. The group of young religious Zionists, like Yosef Burg, had great achievements to their credit. Burg, my closest friend, managed to combine his studies for the rabbinate with much vital chalutzic work. My job was to build up a religious and Zionist youth movement".

What impressed Arieh was that those he trained later became leaders in Jewish communities and in Israel. So many of them, through Bachad, and other bodies, were indeed Arieh's "boys and girls" not only in the kibbutzim but in many responsible communal posts.

And survivors came, with or without the blessing of the British navy, later to become valiant soldiers in Israel's War of Independence.

The rescue work, so dear to Arieh, had been the way he and others could heal, not merely the bodies, but also the minds and souls of those who had suffered so much.

Chapter 9

RESCUE MISSIONS

Having provided a bird's-eye view of this energetic man's career from Magdeburg in 1915 to Jerusalem in 1948, it would not be out of place to give a similar glance at his movements since Independence. The years ahead were full, whether in Britain or Israel, or on his many travels even including Iran. His Jewish idealism, combined with his practical ability, continued with his leading role in Bnei Akiva, Bachad, and Youth Aliyah. His religious Zionism took him into the heart of Hapoel Hamizrachi and leadership of the Mizrachi movement in Britain.

As a Zionist, he was involved too with World Jewish Congress, the Jewish Agency, and the Zionist Actions Committee. There is no end to the list of organisations and issues with which he was connected. He was even a founder of Jewish Childs Day.

Arieh's integrity and devotion to the Jewish faith and people were unimpeachable so that he was universally trusted and respected, indeed held in affection.

These qualities opened doors for him, whether with British Prime Ministers Harold Wilson and Margaret Thatcher, or philanthropists, editors and communal leaders across the broad religious spectrum.

He was a man ever on the move and so often his family came too. After leaving Britain for Israel in 1947, he returned to London in 1956 to dwell in the leafy inner suburb of St. John's Wood. Surprisingly, but at the behest of leading figures in Israel, he had taken on the mantle of director of a bank as well as an earlier position as head of a branch of an Israeli insurance company. He had had no experience in either field but made a success of both. Although he always maintained a home in Israel, he and Henny lived in London for 50 years, returning permanently to Jerusalem in 2006.

Needless to say, Arieh was deeply involved in the many problems of the new state from 1948 to 1956 and his efforts deserve fuller elaboration. However the opportunity statehood presented also provided a challenge. Having seen Israel beat off the major Arab attacks in 1948 and 1949, cynical breaches of the United Nations Resolution and cause of the subsequent refugee problems of both Jews and Arabs, Arieh embarked in the decades ahead on a practical programme of bringing Jews to the Land.

Just as he had toiled for visas for his fellow Jews in Germany and Europe in the 1930s, and after 1945, so he threw himself into the task, for him almost a holy task, of bringing Jews to Israel. This in no way prevented him from taking an active role in the kibbutz movement, nor in communal activities in Britain where he chaired the Israel Committee of the Board of Deputies, but the glowing feature of this restless individual in the years following independence were his endless sojournings to bring in Jews to settle in the Land.

If it took the Children of Israel 40 years to reach the Promised Land, Arieh endeavoured to bring in many thousands in a much shorter time.

It would be opportune therefore in this brief sketch to relate his experiences in Ethiopia, North Africa and the Soviet Union, vastly different places in which dwelt communities with different histories and experiences but all bound together by a deepening consciousness of their Jewish identity.

Chapter 10

THE FALASHAS

It is fascinating to see how the persistent efforts of one man can change public perception and official policy. As far as the Falashas, the Jews of Ethiopia, are concerned, that man was not Arieh Handler but David Kessler. Arieh became his colleague and loyal supporter.

David Kessler, who died at the age of 93 on November 24, 1999, was one of the most unusual men the Anglo-Jewish community produced in many decades. He was the son of Leopold Kessler, (a noted engineer and friend of Theodor Herzl and Chaim Weizmann), who had led the expedition to explore whether El Arish in Sinai was suitable for Jewish settlement. Managing director or chairman of the Jewish Chronicle, which he and his family owned, for almost half a century, David Kessler, despite his reformist Liberal Synagogue views, was determined that every religious opinion within the community should be well and fairly reported. He was shocked by the failure to recognise the rights of Falashas as full and proud Jews.

Kessler was fascinated by the Falashas. Cut off for 2,000 years from the rest of the Jewish people, they clung to the tenets of Biblical Judaism. Some aspects of Judaism were unknown to them. They no longer used the Hebrew language, as the Yemen Jews did. But they retained their distinctiveness from the rest of the Ethiopian population. The very name "Falashas" describes them as "strangers".

Indignant at the failure of Israeli leaders to rescue the Falashas from a country riven by wars and devastated by starvation, Kessler wrote an excellent book about them, "Falashas — the Forgotten Jews of Ethiopia", which won considerable acclaim. This book, and Kessler's chairmanship of the Falasha Welfare Association, did much to influence Jewish and Israeli opinion in favour of recognition of the Falasha as Jews. David Kessler found a determined collaborator in Arieh Handler, as well as Arieh's former colleagues, Lady Henriques, Professor Norman Bentwich, and Samuel (later Lord) Fisher. Those who fought for the Falashas were encouraged by the writings of the 19th century Jewish scholar, Rabbi Dr. Hildesheimer. Kessler and Arieh used his writings in a variety of journals to argue for the validity of the Falasha case. There was stiff opposition from a number of Israeli rabbis. But the trend began to change when the then Sephardi Chief Rabbi of Israel, Ovadia Yosef, pronounced the Falashas genuine Jews, fully entitled thereby to settle in Israel under the Law of Return. This was not the end of the battle. More years were to pass during which the Falashas were requested to undergo a form of conversion, through immersion, before the official rabbinate pronounced them to be entitled to the full rights and obligations of Jews.

Paradoxically the Emperor Haile Selassie's high estimate of the Falashas proved an obstacle to their salvation. When Arieh and Lord Fisher visited Addis Ababa in 1972 to persuade the Emperor to allow the Falashas to leave, they could not shake his conviction that as long as his Jews remained in the country it would prosper. Though disappointed by his arguments, his visitors realised later the point he was making. The Emperor, who bore the title of Lion of Judah and claimed direct descent from King Solomon and Queen Sheba, ended as a prisoner of a brutal Marxist regime and died in a dungeon.

Yet that visit in 1972, by Sammy and Arieh, long remembered, proved most useful. They visited the villages where large numbers of Falashas lived in poor conditions. They were impressed by the little synagogues and delighted to see prayer books sent from Britain and the United States. But officially both Ethiopians and Israelis had to be persuaded as to the movement of the Falashas to Israel.

If there was a single person who could have persuaded the Emperor "to let my people go", it was Sammy Fisher. With an almost Pickwickian figure and smile he was a great persuader. He first came to the notice of the Jewish community, and The Jewish Chronicle, the leading Jewish journal in Britain, by raising funds for Jewish schools and institutions in the

East End of London. But his interests were wider. Winning a Labour seat on a local council, Sammy proved himself a popular champion of the rights of ordinary people, especially of those who were incapable of fighting for themselves. It was not long before he became a Mayor, a highly popular one, winning the support of his Conservative opponents on some notable occasions. Few could fail to be persuaded when Sammy used all his powers. He proved one of the most effective Mayors in East London and Camden. His fellow-Labour Mayors elected him chairman of their association.

It was then that Sammy Fisher attracted the attention of the young Harold Wilson who became leader of the Labour Party and then Prime Minister. They became firm friends and it was through Wilson that Fisher was first made a knight and then a life peer. His tenure as President of the Board of Deputies of British Jews, during which he welcomed the right-wing Likud Prime Minister, Menachem Begin, was considered highly effective. Arieh collaborated closely with him, finding him a man of good sense and one who could always be relied upon to carry through a difficult task. The struggle for the rights and recognition of Ethiopian Jews could be considered among the toughest.

Arieh recalls vividly that visit he and Lord Fisher paid in 1972 to Gondar, the heartland of the Ethiopian Jewish settlement. The visit made a profound and lasting impression on him. Arieh was accompanied by Henny. They had travelled with Sammy Fisher via South Africa.

"We visited the villages around Gondar and were very impressed by the little synagogues and surprised and delighted to see old Polish siddurim, sent by Jews in Poland, as well as those sent by our committee and by Americans. We were greeted by Hebrew songs. We started to badger the Israeli government and Jewish Agency to get those Jews out of the country and into Israel. We knew it was essential that it was done as quickly as possible".

When Arieh and Sammy challenged the Emperor to explain why he did not allow Jews to own land and yet would not allow them to leave, the mystical answer he gave for holding on to the Jews did not convince his Western visitors. But success was at hand. In 1980 20,000 Ethiopian Jews were flown to Israel under "Operation Moses".

In May 1991 came the dramatic news that Israeli aircraft had transported 18,000 Ethiopian Jews to Israel under "Operation Solomon". This came as a great delight to David Kessler and Arieh. Alas, Sammy Fisher was no longer alive to share the joy.

Kessler said: "I was extremely moved by the rescue. It was superbly organised, fantastic. The Israelis were very wise to undertake this wonderful rescue. The anti-government forces in Ethiopia have been encouraged by the Arabs, particularly Colonel Gaddafi. Ethiopian Jews were certainly at risk".

For Arieh, who had just left hospital after an operation, the dramatic news aroused a high enthusiasm. "This is one of the greatest stories ever in Jewish life. What we have seen is of the intensity of Jewish feeling, for Judaism and for Israel. Among the arrivals it was like the beginning of the coming of the Messiah. For me, what happened proves the truth and nobility of Zionism. It has proved also the power of persuasion and dedication of people like David Kessler. When we first started the campaign for the Ethiopian Jews, there were important men in the Israeli Government and the Jewish Agency who said: "Why bother about the Ethiopians? Has not Israel sufficient troubles?" In the end inner pressure, inner conscience, led to this wonderful news of the rescue of our Ethiopian brethren. Yes, I had tears in my eyes when I saw them joyfully, ecstatically, landing on the soil of Israel, their land".

Alas, the Ethiopians' arrival in Israel has not been all joy. Unlike the Yemeni Jews who were transported on what they thought were wings of eagles, in accordance with ancient prophecy, the Ethiopians have not always been able, or, in some cases, not been allowed, to integrate into Israeli society. They emerged from a comparatively primitive society and from tightly-knit communities, in which religious faith was unchallenged, into a raw, rumbustious, modern secular society. Many were not able to adjust, though many others have done so successfully. Perhaps the authorities did not understand the special needs of the black newcomers.

Arieh believed that immense patience and understanding had to be shown to the Ethiopian Jews. He even championed the cause of those

Ethiopian Jews, known as Falash Mura, who, through intimidation and severe pressure, had adopted a form of Christianity but who wished to rejoin their brethren in Israel. These Jews, Arieh pointed out, were neither allowed to own land nor gain employment. It was a forced conversion and they were entitled to say "We are Jews".

Campaigns by Arieh and his friends persuaded the Israeli Government and the Israeli rabbinate to adopt a more merciful attitude to the converted Jews. A number of them were allowed to settle in Israel, re-adopt Judaism and rejoin their families. Yet, for Arieh, the situation of Ethiopian Jews remained a cause for anxiety. About 60,000 Falashas had arrived in Israel under Operations Moses and Solomon since 1970 but a number were still far away from the country of their dreams – for a variety of reasons. Two thousand Ethiopian immigrants staged a protest outside Prime Minister Netanyahu's office in Jerusalem in July 1998. They demanded that the government should bring in 5,000 of their relatives who, they claimed, were still stranded in Ethiopia. The protest followed the revelation that the Israeli government had closed a transit camp near Addis Ababa and had decided not to admit any more Ethiopians who did not qualify under the Law of Return. The last 20 of the 4,000 Falash Mura, who had been in the transit camp for seven years, were flown to Israel for humanitarian reasons. Perhaps carrying out a protest meeting qualified them as true Israelis!

Arieh made efforts to help all the newcomers. He realised their potential. He arranged for a number to settle in a village near Haifa, named after Orde Wingate, a British military hero in Israel's history, and for others to live in a village close to Kibbutz Lavi, where Arieh long had had connections.

His view that patience was vital has, he now feels, been justified. In his 90s, he points out with pride Falasha youngsters in universities, in the Army, in teaching, in industry, gradually integrating in the many cultures that make up the melting pot of Israel.

He recalls with enthusiasm the efforts of Sammy Fisher and the small London Committee, but gives full praise to the leadership of David Kessler. This story illustrates another aspect of Arieh's character. He had so often been the initiator of activities, playing a leading role but, in this case, he was happy to be one of a team in achieving the required result.

Provided the object was to further the Jewish cause, Arieh was always a good team player.

Chapter 11

OUT OF AFRICA

Based after 1947 in Israel, deeply involved in what was happening in the new State, nevertheless he never forgot his mission to bring Jews to Israel. And so began the work of rescuing North African Jewry.

With the ending of the Second World War and the establishment of Israel, Arieh went on several trips to Africa and Asia. His task was to meet Jewish communities and discuss with them the possibilities of emigration to Israel.

One of the journeys took him to Tangiers and to areas in Morocco. His main task was to contact Moroccan Jews as an emissary of Zalman Shragai, head of the Aliyah Department of the Jewish Agency. Just as David Kessler figured so prominently in the Falasha story, so did Shragai influence Arieh in the rescue of North African Jews. Zalman Shragai was a remarkable man. Learned and religious, with a small black beard and piercing eyes, he was a formidable personality. He had a high role in the Mizrachi movement in which Arieh was active. He was an able organiser and administrator. He was also a determined Zionist. In his religious life he was attached to the Radziner Chassidim. It was a Radziner Rebbe who at the end of the 19th century rediscovered the fish that provided the dye for the tchelet, the blue fringe in the tzizit worn by religious Jews. Arieh worked with all religious groups, from Chassidim to Progressive Jews. He was, in a way, a man for all seasons and for all movements.

Arieh greatly admired Shragai. He realised that there could not be a more dedicated man and leader in the struggle, dangerous at times, to gather the dispersed Jews in every corner of the world and bring them to Israel.

Moroccan Jews had gone through several dramatic crises during their long history, in which they took pride, a sentiment which has prevailed to this day and has even had a later political significance in Israel. They lived in Morocco in comparative freedom when it was a Roman province but their situation deteriorated when the Roman Empire became Christian. All synagogues were destroyed in the seventh century under Byzantine rule."Love one another as I have loved you"stated Jesus the Jew, a teaching his followers conveniently forgot.

After the Arab conquest, the communities increased in number, with Fez and Sigilmessa becoming famous Jewish seats of learning including the home, for a period, of Maimonides. However the ban on Judaism proclaimed by the fanatical Almohades rulers in the 12th and 13th centuries brought an end to this golden period, but, on their fall, Jewish communities again prospered. Refugees arrived from Spain in considerable numbers at the end of the 14th century. Even larger numbers came from Spain in 1492 in the face of the iniquitous Inquisition when the Jews were expelled from the country. It is historically fascinating that in Toledo in 1992 the Spaniards publicly apologised to the Jews of the world, but it took 500 years!

However the situation in Morocco again deteriorated. Jews were ill-treated, confined to their own areas, compelled to wear distinctive black clothing and were, occasionally, the object of physical attacks. Despite these conditions a number of Jews did, from time to time, rise to high positions in the State as treasurers and agents for Sultans, but they generally ended as victims. The situation particularly deteriorated for the Jews under the Rashid dynasty from the late 17th century. A mission to ameliorate the Jewish plight carried out in the 19th century by the renowned philanthropist, Sir Moses Montefiore, proved ineffective. Only when the French took over the country's administration in 1912 was order re-established, violence against the Jewish population stopped and the status of Jews improved. Similar favourable conditions prevailed in the Spanish zone. Jews were also prominent in the international port of Tangiers.

When the exciting news arrived in Morocco that the Jewish State had been proclaimed on May 14, 1948, many Jews, faced with growing anti-

Jewish feelings around them, found their way to Israel to settle. Moroccan Jews had largely remained faithful to their religious faith and all were immensely proud of their great scholars. Some also went to France and Canada when the opportunity arose, but most found homes in the new State.

When Arieh set out to organise aliyah from Morocco, he found a sizeable community which Israel urgently needed to absorb. A census taken in 1960 showed that there were 160,000 Jews in Morocco. Five years later this number had declined to 75,000. By 1973 the number had been reduced to 31,000, and by 1990 there were only 10,000 Jews left in the whole country. The late King Hassan made many appeals to Moroccan Jews living in Israel and other countries to return as they were urgently needed to modernise the country. Few heeded his call. Arieh thus had a formidable task in front of him when he first arrived in Casablanca in 1952. The Israeli government under Ben-Gurion made every effort to encourage immigration for North Africans, working closely with religious and non-religious groups.

"In Morocco my main job was to get in touch with leading Jews in the large cities – Casablanca, Marrakesh, Tangiers, among others", Arieh recalls. "Instead of staying in a hotel in Tangiers, which might have caused me problems, I stayed at the home of the parents of the Reichmann brothers who later became famous as financiers and builders of the huge Canary Wharf complex in London. After spending some ten days in Morocco arranging for future immigrants to settle in Israel, I flew in a small plane from Tangiers to Madrid". He was constantly on the move.

Arieh recalls: "I have to stress that German immigration to Israel was very, very important but I also take satisfaction in the rescue work among North African Jews. To this day I am in touch with North African Jews who immigrated to Israel, many of them now elderly people. And I also came to know their sons. One of them is the successful Mayor and politician, Elli Dayan – not connected with the Moshe Dayan family – whose parents came from Morocco". The children of North African Jews were also his "boys and girls". He added:

"Bringing North African Jews to Israel was a great achievement, much greater than most people realise. It was accomplished because we all worked closely together. There was complete cooperation between religious and non-religious officials. We all pulled together in the same direction, I was the main official as far as religious immigration was concerned but the non-religious officials worked just as hard and with the same dedication". This also applied to his efforts in both Tunisia and Libya. He was especially fascinated by the 'Jewish' island of Djerba.

One of the most notable men Arieh worked with in Paris was Akiva Levinsky, Jewish Agency treasurer, whom he described as a "very fine man". Although Levinsky was a non-religious Jew he worked in total amity with Arieh. They appreciated each other's qualities. After one personal mishap, Levinsky said to Arieh: "You are one of the few who came to see me after my accident". Typical! This successful cooperation between religious and non-religious Jews on aspects of problems which involved them all, so notable in Germany and in the work for immigration to Israel, made a profound impression on Arieh. This success, he says, is one of the main reasons why he always sought cooperation with all groups, whether in Anglo-Jewry or elsewhere, for the common good.

This was Arieh Handler, both leader and team player. The emergence of the State of Israel and the defeat of the Arab onslaught only increased antagonism against Jews in the Arab world. Arieh recognised that the North African communities faced an increasingly dangerous future, especially with the rise of Arab nationalism.

For most Jews, despite their contribution to those countries over many years, danger signals were flashing alarmingly. There was no future for them and their children in the highly charged atmosphere. Attacks on them took place, but security and hope beckoned in Israel, and so, in their thousands, they made their way there. Arieh was one of the catalysts, a major one, that made this aliyah possible. Once again, this 'non-stop' man used all his energy in a different kind of rescue, and succeeded.

He might note with interest that it took a further 50 years, in 2008, for procedures to be adopted to seek compensation for Jewish property left in North African countries. Whether that campaign for justice succeeds cannot yet be foreseen, but certainly Arieh could sit back, not that he ever would, and be grateful that, once again, he had been able to do his duty to his people.

Chapter 12

EXODUS FROM RUSSIA

Moses led over 600,000 Children of Israel to freedom out of the house of bondage. Arieh Handler, also in a position of leadership, alongside others, led a decade-long campaign that helped to release over a million Jews from the iron grip of Soviet dictatorship. It is a story that does him honour and which had a radical effect on the future of Israel. His role was played out, not from Tel Aviv or Jerusalem, but from London. What was this wandering Zionist doing in the British capital?

From 1947 to 1956 he and his family lived in Israel, with Arieh deeply involved in his political and communal work. But then Dr. Barth, director of Bank Leumi, asked Arieh to open, in London, a branch of Migdal, an insurance company owned by the bank. Arieh declined, saying he knew nothing about insurance. At the time, his hero Ben-Gurion had given up political power for a new role as a farmer, a kibbutznik, in the Negev settlement of Sde Boker.

The new Prime Minister was Moshe Sharett, who shared with Henny a love of music. It was Sharett who told Arieh, almost ordered him, that he should go to London, as a duty. So, off he went, with his family, learned about insurance, and made a success of the company. The good fairy had never left him.

As if that were not enough, Dr. Tibor Rosenbaum, who had created the International Credit Bank in Geneva, asked Arieh to head a branch of the bank in London. "But I know nothing about banking" protested this leader of Hapoel Hamizrachi. However the same influence was brought to bear, and it was not long before Arieh opened the bank's modest office in St. Swithin's Lane in the City of London, next door to the imposing bank of the House of Rothschild. Arieh made a success too of the branch and so he became a banker.

Clearly, for whatever reason, the man, devoted to Israel, found London had become the centre of his activities for years ahead.

Residing in London, he continued to be involved in Mizrachi Bachad, Bnei Akiva and also became a Deputy in the Board of Deputies, actively concerned especially in its links with Israel.

At the time, there were stirrings among the Jews of the Soviet Union. Winston Churchill had spoken of the Iron Curtain that separated the Communist dictatorships of Eastern Europe from the democracies of the West. And those dictatorships bore heavily on the life of Jews. They had suffered greatly when the Germans invaded Russia in 1941. The Nazis, in their bestial brutality, had murdered hundreds of thousands of Jews, typified by the grim massacre of Babi Yar in the Ukraine. The Germans were the enemy and so Jews loyally served in the Soviet army as well as joining the heroic Partisans in the woods.

The war over, Stalin-led anti-Semitism remained, in fact grew, in the Soviet Union. The KGB secret service and the anti-Zionists in the Communist Yevsectia continued to persecute Jews. Arieh and his colleagues in London watched anxiously.

In Russia, in past times there had arisen the famous Chassidim of the 18th century, the Baal Shem Tov, Dov Baer, and the mystic Nachman of Bratslav. From Russia, in the 19th and 20th centuries, there had emerged a golden burst of Yiddish and Hebrew poetry, the creativity of Bialik, Peretz and Tchernikovsky, whose striking words echoed in Jewish souls.

Throughout the Communist regime from 1917, there existed a form of militant atheism, yet, in a quite extraordinary way, although largely underground, the Jewish and Zionist spirit remained. Groups had somehow met in the 1920s and 1930s and, despite the loss to Judaism of many younger Jews, an older generation held on, especially fortified by knowledge of the newly-arisen Jewish State.

In October 1948, Golda Meir, Israel's first Ambassador to Moscow, appeared there in the main synagogue. 50,000 Jews welcomed her! This reflected the longing for Zion that remained deep-down despite all the authorities could do. A writer in Chayenu, of which Arieh had been editor, stated:

"I learned of youth brought up under Soviet conditions and yet loyal to the national ideas of the Jews. I heard of the indescribably difficult road of the Zionist youth, fighting with unusual sacrifice for the ideals of Zionism, even facing wholesale arrests".

By the 1950s thousands of Jews all over Russia applied for exit visas to Israel. The applications were refused. Many applicants, including noted scientists, lost their jobs. The word `Refusenik' began to be heard. Arieh went to Moscow. He saw how the activists were jailed, often on false charges, as in the case of Anatole (later Natan) Sharansky, whose name, as he lay in prison, became a symbol of the fight for freedom. Another description emerged for the persecuted Jews. They became the "Prisoners of Zion".

Arieh and his colleagues inside and outside the Board were deeply concerned. They called on the Soviet Ambassador in his palatial London Embassy to protest. There was no response. With the backing of his friend, Sammy Fisher, then President of the Board, colleagues like Sir Sigmund Sternberg, Alex Margulies, Barnett and Greville Janner, a new organisation came into being, the National Council for Soviet Jewry. Arieh became its Vice-Chairman.

With his usual energy, he ensured that the body soon became influential. It publicised the plight of Soviet Jews widely in Britain, in schools and universities, among politicians. It involved in its work many synagogues and Jewish organisations. It co-operated with similar bodies in the USA and elsewhere. Arieh always made it clear that the Council was not against the Soviet government but only wanted to help Soviet Jews. In fact he had good relations with Soviet officials. He received advice from fellow-Labourite, Harold Wilson and also from Conservative Prime Minister, Margaret Thatcher.

The mass signing of a petition was launched in London. Mrs. Thatcher came to add her signature, alongside many Jews and non-Jews. A conference of world Jewish leaders was arranged in London, with Edgar Bronfman, Isy Liebler, and others. Mrs. Thatcher welcomed them to Downing Street.

The campaign grew with, as Arieh noted, 100% support from the British government. A major march and rally of many thousands took place, in and around Hyde Park, solidly supported by British Jews. Arieh's enthusiasm and organisational ability came to the fore again, assisted by Chairman, June Jacobs.

In the Soviet Union, the leadership changed. A new man arose, Mikhail Gorbachov. He was cast in a different mould from his mentally arthritic predecessors. He went to Iceland to meet American President Ronald Reagan. He was not the only one who went to Iceland. Arieh went there too, hoping to present the case for exit permits for the Refuseniks to the Soviet President.

Gradually international pressure grew on Mr. Gorbachov, not least from Margaret Thatcher, and finally permission to leave was granted. Almost one million Soviet Jews left for Israel, a huge aliyah, many with scientific and academic abilities, destined to have a tremendous effect on the future of the country. The campaign had been successful.

Arieh knew that, as with the Falashas, the Moroccan Jews, the earlier German Jews, it would require patience and understanding to absorb and integrate the new and powerful wave of immigration. It would take time for the newcomers to adjust to the `feel' of the country, the Hebrew language, the dynamism. He knew that among the Russian Jews were men and women of distinction and ability, and he worked hard to help them in the absorption process. Gradually that process took place, as Arieh later happily noted.

The National Council for Soviet Jewry was yet another vehicle for yet another campaign to free his people from forms of bondage, enabling them to develop themselves as individuals, and for the greater ideal of Israel and the Jewish people. Arieh never wavered in his devotion to that people and to Zionism, whenever Jews were afflicted and needed help.

Moses may have changed the nature of the staff he held in his hand. Arieh never changed the single-mindedness of his mission but, like his Biblical predecessor, he changed the lives of so many he led with distinction from servitude to freedom.

Chapter 13

LOOKING BACK

Arieh Handler sits comfortably in his airy second floor apartment in Kiryat Moshe, a largely orthodox district in Jerusalem. Occasionally a soft breeze wafts through the open glass doors, a cool breath amidst the enveloping warmth of the summer sun. Glasses perched on his nose, Arieh is invariably reading. He has been reading all his life. He has been loyal to The Economist, the famous British weekly. Daily he scans The Jerusalem Post in English, other weeklies and dailies in Hebrew, and, from Britain, The Jewish Chronicle, and the Jewish News. He points out the journal of the Association of Jewish Refugees, whose words are especially meaningful to him.

The telephone rings continually. Old friends in Israel want to know if he is well. Old friends in London, like the late Lady Jakobovits and Israel Finestein Q.C. also want to know if he is well. There are not so many contemporaries of this 95 year-old still about, but those who remain keep in touch, as do his children and grandchildren. His 'boys and girls' of old are spread around Israel and constantly wish him well. A visit to an Old People's residential home results in a parade of admirers shaking hands with him. They are delighted to see this 'grand old man', who remembers them and recalls events well over half-a-century before.

There are visitors from abroad, individuals, professors, but also groups on study tours of Israel, who ask him to speak to them. Arieh is living history. His life summarises graphically the Jewish story of the 20th century, with its tragedy, success, heartaches, and courage. One day some academic will take a year off and produce a comprehensive study of the life of this man, with a further volume containing extracts from the mass of his collected original documents.

Arieh is rarely alone, so often the problem of the elderly. A resident

Filipino looks after his needs, his food, his pills, conscientiously. She even accompanies him to and from the local synagogue on Friday nights and Saturday mornings. Although he walks slowly – the knees are not what they were – he walks regularly, to prayers, to the shops, to the doctor.

His family are all around him, from Danny who lives in London, but who constantly phones and regularly visits, from Gabriel (Gaby) who is present daily, when he is not teaching in Tel Aviv University. Grandchildren, great-grandchildren are always about. There are weddings, Barmitzvahs, birthdays, as well as candles alight, remembering.

And Arieh remembers, especially Henny, his wife for 66 years. They returned to Israel from London in 2006 but sadly Henny passed away in August 2007. Their lives had been intertwined, devoted, complementing each others' qualities and strengths.

Arieh has always been devoted to mainstream Orthodoxy in Judaism, but in his efforts to serve and save his fellow-Jews, he had worked closely with non-orthodox Jews, Conservative, Reform, Progressive, secular Jews, but he never departed from traditional Judaism. He always wore a kippa on his head. Grace was always said after meals, often with a Mishnaic or Talmudic contribution from Chabad-attached Gaby.

Festivals are highlights, as are also Israel's Independence Day and special days.

This attachment to the religion gives a structure to his life, even a purpose and a hope. He had achieved the dream of Tevye in Fiddler on the Roof, for Arieh has an honoured seat by the Eastern wall in the synagogue facing the congregation. Tevye's song "Tradition, tradition" could aptly apply to him.

As he sits at home and remembers, there is much to recall, people, places, events, organisations. Of the latter, there were at least twenty in which he played an active and significant role. He finds it difficult to choose the most important ones, but when pressed, he refers especially to Bachad, the movement of religious pioneers, to Youth Aliyah, of which he was director, bringing young people, whether religious or not, to Israel, and to the National Council for Soviet Jewry, which helped to open doors for a million people, changing their lives and, in many ways Israel itself.

All the organisations held him in high esteem. In 1999 Bnei Akiva produced a book of Prayers and Songs. These words are in the Foreword:

"We have celebrated 60 years in Britain. We dedicate our book as an expression of our gratitude to the individual who has devoted his life to Bnei Akiva. He has dedicated his life to the Movement. Arieh, you are a true visionary. You are an inspiration".

Inspiration, visionary! Arieh would have waved aside those words. He was only doing his duty. He could take pride in his achievement, but pride was not for him. He simply did what he felt he had to do.

Every one of the twenty organisations could write a similar testimony to his work for their cause. A word he often mentioned with a smile was Thaxted. He smiles because this was where young Jews were prepared, in England – hachshara is the word – for agricultural work in Israel after 1945. Thaxted is a delightful, historic, sleepy village in Essex, but, in the farm Arieh and others had established, there was intense enthusiasm and activity as city dwellers learned the ways of pioneers, on the land, chalutzim. And Thaxted was but one of several such farms in Britain.

Of course, the next step after the farms were the religious kibbutzim, the communal agricultural settlements in Israel. He had a hand in the setting-up and development of several, but his real love was Lavi, which he and Henny visited often.

If he were asked to name particular friends, out of a long list, he would refer to Dr. Yosef Burg, "like a brother to me", Moshe Unna, David Bet-Arieh and Rudi Herz, all devoted workers for the kibbutz movement, all achieving prominence later in life.

This capacity for friendship is one of his greatest qualities allied to a genuine modesty. People liked him. In those grim earlier days, the Gestapo had allowed him to travel in and out of Germany in pursuit of visas, an almost unheard-of thing. But all those in contact with Arieh felt the warmth and sincerity of his character. This extended to British Prime Ministers, to Israeli Prime Ministers, and to everyone, at all levels of society with whom he came into contact. It is why visitors from abroad naturally make their way to his home.

He did indeed meet many people on his travels. Almost as an aside, he mentions his journeys throughout the United States, post-war, as world director of Hapoel Hamizrachi, speaking to communities from New York to Chicago to San Francisco, explaining Israel's needs and seeking support.

Arieh Handler knew many and was known to many. The list of his acquaintances and friends is seemingly endless. They include a host of Chief Rabbis – Hertz, Brodie, Jakobovits, Sacks, Unterman, Lau, as well as Rabbi Louis Jacobs. Personalities known to him included Harold Wilson, Margaret Thatcher, Tony Blair, King Hussein of Jordan, Sarah Churchill, daughter of Winston, and many others. Of Israeli leaders, he mentions Yitzhak Rabin, Shimon Peres, but his greatest admiration remains for David Ben-Gurion, a man made in an heroic mould.

In the 21st century he looks back with nostalgia to people of the quality of Ben-Gurion and Moshe Sharett. He does not find their equivalent in the modern Knesset. Few political leaders of a later period possess a comparable sense of history and vision. That may also be the mark of other nations, but it is a source of regret to Arieh.

There are certain dates that are uppermost in his mind, of course his marriage, the birth of their children, and especially that day in May 1948 when independence was declared. But he goes back even further. When he was 13 he attended a local Gymnasium, a school that impressed him as did, at the age of 14, the Lessing Gymnasium school, years of study in a yeshiva, apart from the endless Latin and Greek, remain vividly in his mind.

It is well nigh impossible to sum up the many lives of Arieh, his many worlds. Here was a kibbutz enthusiast and founder who was also a banker. Here was a deeply religious soul who was a practical man of the world. Here was a man who co-operated closely with non-orthodox Jews, for their common cause, yet never compromised his orthodoxy. Here was a family man, devoted indeed to all generations, who was late for his own wedding and spent much of his life away from home, travelling from country to country. Here was an editor of journals, a prolific reader of journals, but essentially a man of action. Here was a political being yet whose activities never extended to the Knesset as a member or even a local town hall. Above all here was a Jew, with a mission, inspired by his faith, who saved the lives of so many and also brought so many to the land that he loved.

Chapter 14

LOOKING FORWARD

With a face always on the verge of a smile, Arieh Handler sits back in a comfortable chair, ready to answer questions. He is used to answering questions. He had a host of them from the world's media in May 2008. His power of recall is amazing despite his 94 years, as he adjusts the kippa on his head and responds thoughtfully. He is impressed with what has been done in Israel. There are some wonderful people in the Land, especially many of those he helped to bring, and their children. He would like them to be more active as leaders.

Arieh touched on the subject close to his heart. He thinks back to Ben-Gurion, even to Arthur Ruppin, "Ruppin knew little Hebrew but was a great Zionist, an example, a major educational factor, the type of man the country needs".

The question of leadership dominates his mind. Leadership in Israel, indeed in the whole world, is not what it should be. "Many things now direct the attention of young people. We must make a special effort to avert future problems". That comment applies to all political and religious streams, for Arieh is very much a "one nation" person.

He realises the problems, the electoral system, the way politicians look inward rather than at the broader picture. He casts his mind back to Rabbi Soloveichek, Rabbi Leo Baeck and others. "I knew them all". Some declined to come to Israel. They confessed that they did not feel strong enough to lead the Jewish people in their own land. Arieh acknowledges, "we are not an easy nation. You have to be very strong to lead this people".

But he remains optimistic that the right kind of leadership will emerge.

A smile covers his face as he approves of what has been achieved in Israel. "Thousands who had no hope or any chance where they were as

Jews now have a chance to develop". This modest man never even hints that those thousands may have had such a chance because of his efforts.

He is pleased that the country has developed physically and become a real nation. Integration has been gradual. Knowledge of the Hebrew language and service in the Army have helped, but there remains a need to create a country of equals. We want "to create honesty, integrity, knowledge, and scholarship".

As for religion it was important to recognise that there are different views, "but we are all Jews". He is concerned over religious groups who live "in separate worlds, a life on their own", contrasting, them with the outgoing, all-embracing approach of Chief Rabbi Kook. People should have their eyes and ears open to those of a different persuasion.

He is full of praise for Israelis in the fields of industry, finance and technology. "We have fine people here in every sphere of economic life. There is a tremendous possibility". Israel could do so much for the betterment of the whole region and of other countries further afield. He appreciates that many gifted Israelis spend time abroad and so contribute to the well-being of other nations.

Pondering for a moment on his late wife Henny's musical ability, he is glad that there are many Israelis gifted in music and the arts. Arieh himself is not a musician, nor, as was made clear years ago, a singer.

He adjusts his position in the chair and thinks of broader pictures. Looking at the world he hopes Israel will create stronger links with India and China, but also remain in close contact with smaller countries.

As for the Arab world, Israel has to work hard to find a common language that would lead to peace. He ends his reflections and hopes with the words: "Even when I was young I was always positive about the future of our people and Israel, so, even with our present problems, I remain an optimist about the future".

He sits back again, satisfied with his remark. O! If only this man were sixty years younger, what could he not do!!

POSTSCRIPT - JUNE 2009

I sit with Arieh. He is in bed. He had two falls, is bruised all over. No fun at 94. One eye is almost closed, his right arm and right side are black with injuries. The broken ribs will mend, say the medical world, but occasionally the mending hurts.

He talks about his late wife, Henny, talks to her, and others. The mind wanders. Danny, his son from London, stays several weeks. Gaby, his other son, a Tel Aviv University professor, is on hand daily. Others look in constantly. Medi, the Filipino carer, is pure gold. She shops, she cooks, she cares for the patient night and day.

I am here for two weeks, to complete this sketch. Gradually the imaginary figures depart and Arieh is back with us. He studies the photographs, can recall every face, can put a name to every face. He begins to hazard a joke. A shy smile haunts his lips.

We discuss old times. Visitors from Lavi, the kibbutz he helped found, rush to see their friend and discuss even older times, way back when this buoyant settlement began.

We spend the day in splendid Shaare Zedek hospital. He is leaned over by white coats and tested for this and that. Nothing. His doctor calls, surprised at his improvement, comments on a strong constitution. Behold this man Arieh Handler, all of a piece, his long life full. He tells me that if he had been able to save but one life, it would all have been worthwhile. How many owe their lives to this one man, who never condemns, judges, reproves, but always smiles? May the good Lord smile on him and give him health and peace.

TRIBUTES

The following pages contain a selection of tributes to Arieh sent to me. I hope those who wrote them will not chastise me either for not including all their words or for considerably reducing them. To include them in their entirety would have meant another book, whilst I have no doubt there are many others, whom I have not approached, but who would have added particular and pertinent comments.

I believe though that what follows is representative of the many different aspects of Arieh's life. They are not set out in any particular order.

YOUTH ALIYAH

Arieh Handler is, indeed, an outstanding man amongst his equals. He devoted his life to the welfare and care of others, and his devotion to the children of Youth Aliyah Child Rescue is legendary.

As one of the founder members of the original Youth Aliyah Committee for Great Britain and Eire, he was instrumental in contributing his first-hand knowledge of what the children, rescued from war-torn Europe, had actually gone through. His personal experience with these youngsters meant a great deal to them, of course, but also to all those who were privileged enough to work with him.

When I first met Arieh, I was overawed by his sense of purpose and his deep belief that the children in the care of our 5 Youth Aliyah villages in Israel had the unspoken right to a future as fully fledged citizens, leaving behind their traumatic childhood.

"The children come first" was Arieh's maxim, and one we continually strive to carry through today.

Adrienne Sussman

MICHAEL FREEDLAND
A truly, lovely great man.

ISRAEL FINESTEIN Q.C.
One senses from this book, how naturally and deeply this stalwart of religious Zionism has in practice been a loyal devotee of those golden rules prescribed by our great sages. "Receive all people" declared Shammai, "with a cheerful countenance".

Always a man of firm principle, Arieh long seemed to be the community's born conciliator. How often have we heard in the midst of communal discord his calming voice and mediating counsel. All parties have shown confidence in his wisdom and experience.

His self-appointed and at times dangerous double mission has been to save Jewish lives physically and to advance especially among the young the knowledge and the spirit of our Hebraic traditions. This was his Zionism – a vital political movement for the re-establishment of Jewish statehood on democratic and equitable lines in the ancestral home.

Xenophobia and chauvinism in any form have always been alien to this man. True to his name, Arieh has readily displayed the courage of a lion in upholding what he deemed to be right.

In short compass and without affectation Aubrey well recounts the truly remarkable life of a personality whose faith, through thick and thin, and whose talent for friendship are undimmed with age.

ASSOCIATION OF JEWISH REFUGEES (A.J.R.)

Arieh Handler has devoted his whole life to helping Jewish communities in need. But we need particularly to commend him for his invaluable services to the young Jewish refugees from Germany and Austria who came to the UK in the late 1930s. As the head of Bachad, the religious Zionist Movement, he worked relentlessly to set up and run training centres (Hachsharot) in the whole of Britain, such as Whittingehame and Gwrych Castle. Through the devoted work of Arieh Handler, many young people gained a sense of solidarity and purpose in difficult times, which helped them to settle into their new surroundings and overcome the difficulties of their traumatic journeys. Arieh Handler's unfaltering commitment to helping Jewish refugees from Nazi Europe, and later Russian and Ethiopian Jews, is a true inspiration for future generations.

Michael Newman

ELDRED TABACHNIK Q.C.

Arieh Handler is a significant and memorable figure in the history of British Jewry, with long service to the Jewish community. He was present at the signing of Israel's Declaration of Independence. His entire life has been centred around the establishment, progress, and future of the Jewish State. It is an objective to which he has contributed a lifetime of strenuous work.

He was always a devoted Jewish activist and played a prominent role in the British Jewish community. As a member of the Board of Deputies of British Jews he spoke up for what he fervently believed and was always fair and balanced.

I also knew Arieh in the context of British Friends of Boys Town, Jerusalem. No matter how busy he was, he always tried to attend the meetings and offered sound advice, which was always constructive and relevant.

May he be blessed at least for a hundred and twenty years! I, and all my colleagues active in Jewish affairs, wish Arieh a long and happy life.

GAIL SEAL

I remember as a young child, my late father, Archie Lew, telling me about his dear friend Arieh Handler and the fact he was the only person he knew that had been in the audience when David Ben-Gurion declared Israel as a state. As I grew up I was aware that Arieh was a great friend of my family and very close to my uncle, Dayan Dr. J. Lew.

When I became the President of JNF, Arieh was one of the first to write to me and congratulate me. He was proud of the fact that I was the first woman to head up a 100 year-old British charity. When there were difficulties Arieh used to call me to offer advice and guidance. I always took it. He was a wise and elegant counsellor. When he went to live in Israel he continued to call and we had many interesting discussions on politics and life in the Diaspora and life in Israel.

Arieh was a star and will always be remembered by me as a friend and confidant.

PROFESSOR COLIN SHINDLER

Arieh Handler is a living symbol of the supreme effort that twentieth century Jews made to establish the state of Israel in the most adverse of circumstances. There are few people in 2009 who can personally recall the founding fathers of the state and bring the dramatic events of 1948 to life once more. Arieh is the last survivor of that small band of men and women who gathered together in May 1948 to hear Ben-Gurion proclaim the establishment of a state of Israel in the Land of Israel, in all of 32 minutes. That was on a Friday afternoon. Arieh went to shul shortly afterwards to welcome the arrival of Shabbat amidst the sound of Egyptian bombers dropping their payloads on the worshippers.

Arieh's vision of religious Zionism as a member of Hapoel Hamizrachi is one that he passionately believes in and lives by. It is one that might not be recognised by the less enlightened in Israel and in the Golah today. His personal commitment to the campaign for Soviet Jewry helped many to secure their liberation. Few can attain the heights of his contribution, but all Hovevei Zion should aspire to it.

118

FLO KAUFMANN

Arieh became something of a mentor to me over the years, and encouraged me in my communal career. Only last January, I invited him to attend the meeting of the World Jewish Congress held in Jerusalem, as part of the Board delegation which I had the privilege of leading. It gave me a real thrill when he was introduced as the last survivor who had been "in the room" when Israel's Declaration of Independence was signed. Arieh really is a piece of living history and knowing him is my own personal link with the establishment of the State of Israel. Long may he continue to lead an active life in Israel, and be well in his retirement.

LADY JAKOBOVITS

With a heart full of gratitude to Hashem for Arieh's life and the blessing of a wonderful relationship that both my dear husband Rav Lord Jakobovits and I have enjoyed with him for many decades. Arieh Handler has always been one of the most colourful, enchanting and creative characters in the life of anyone who knew and knows him.

Arieh, with his unique foresight, was a founder of many youth organisations, which to this day fulfil his hopes as their young women and men are wholeheartedly and cheerfully committed to the State of Israel. I write these few loving thoughts about Arieh and congratulate every one of the participants in the publication of this book, which I am sure will be of great interest and give much joy to many a reader.

LORD JANNER OF BRAUNSTONE Q.C. (GREVILLE JANNER)

I have known, respected and been very fond of Arieh Handler all my life. He is a unique man, not only for his public work, but as a friend and joyful companion and colleague.

I was especially happy to work with him on the Board of Deputies and on the National Council for Soviet Jewry. His good nature, energy and total focus on the essentials of our particular efforts were always an example to all of us.

Bis 120!

JEWISH CHILDS DAY

Arieh Handler is the founding father of Jewish Childs Day and has been a true inspiration to the charity ever since. His passion for helping young people was evident at every grant allocations meeting, which he attended until he made Aliyah at the age of 90. Even now he reviews the applications with great detail and discusses them over the telephone from Israel.

Arieh's memory of events and his stories of how he started the charity remain as vivid as ever and his understanding of the challenges and opportunities for Jewish children is exceptional. His love of Israel burns as strongly today as it did in JCD's birth year of 1947.

Mrs. Joy Moss

PROFESSOR GEOFFREY ALDERMAN

Arieh Handler is one of the great Jewish heroes of modem times. Oblivious to any personal danger he risked his life many times in order to rescue Jews from the clutches of the Nazis. Simultaneously, as a Zionist, he played a central role in the re-establishment of the Jewish state. Later, he contributed to the governance of that state – Israel. But he also immersed himself in the culture and politics of the United Kingdom – his temporary home – and in the life of its Jewish minority. His achievements serve as an inspiration, and as a proof of the enduring tenacity of the Jewish people.

PROFESSOR ERIC MOONMAN OBE

Arieh Handler has been a cornerstone of the Jewish community in Britain and Israel for all the years I can remember. Two things stand out in my mind. He and I were involved some years ago in attempting to merge the two Zionist Federations in Britain. Meetings were called two or three times a day for weeks on end to satisfy everyone' s point of view. He was a valuable ally and he joked at the time that I was seeing more of him than his wife and family. Eventually, our efforts were successful and I realised then what a great team-player his is.

Secondly, Arieh was able to diffuse most of the problems that come the way of a national leader. He attracts love and affection and a way of life which I have tried to emulate.

GEOFFREY PAUL

As a young Jewish journalist trying to find his way around the community, there were times when it seemed that a whole pixie-load of Arieh Handlers not only ran but also populated Anglo-Jewry. Turn up at any meeting, from the Deputies to a rally somewhere in the provinces in support of Israel, and there – full flow – was Arieh Handler. Pop down to an Essex training farm where young men and women were readying for agricultural settlement in Israel and there was Arieh Handler. It seemed no matter what shul you attended, which charity committee you dropped in on or even whichever dinner party you were invited to, there he was, smiling, voluble, ever more reasonable than anyone else and ready always to expound on the issue at hand, or any other. Like many in this community I learned a lot about Jewish commitment, about ahavat Israel, from Arieh Handler and remain indebted to him to this day.

LORD MICHAEL LEVY

I have had the pleasure and privilege of knowing Arieh Handler for many years. He is a former Bnei Akiva member, as am I.

His commitment and dedication to the Jewish people and his love for Israel is truly outstanding.

Arieh has always conducted himself in a dignified manner and has endeared himself to so many different segments within the Angle-Jewish community.

Arieh has been a shining example for so many. Anglo-Jewry has been enriched by having had him involved for so many years in such an active way in our community.

Israel is now blessed to have him living in his beloved country.

With deep respect and immense admiration to a very special friend, to a very special Jew and to a very dignified leader.

ZIONIST FEDERATION

Arieh Handler is one of the most extraordinary people I have had the privilege of knowing.

His life reflects and is intimately bound up with the Jewish experience of the last 80 years.

I was not born when he travelled with a Gestapo passport to rescue kids on the Kindertransport nor when he founded Bnei Akiva nor in his early days with Mizrachi, nor when he was one of the 200 invited guests to hear the Declaration of Israeli Independence being announced on May 14th 1948. We first worked closely together in the days of fighting for the release of Soviet Jewry. He was Vice-Chairman of the UK National Council for Soviet Jewry when I was Chairman. His knowledge, contacts and experience were unrivalled. He had the confidence both of those who agreed with him and those we had to influence who might not have agreed. There are many Soviet Jews who obtained their freedom and came to Israel through his work. I still see him at Zionist events in Israel.

I do not know anyone from across the political and religious spectrum in Britain, Europe and Israel who does not have the highest regard for Arieh and what he has achieved in a remarkable life.

Hazach Baruch.

Andrew Balcombe (Chairman)

SIR SIGMUND STERNBERG

I remember Arieh Handler when he was a madrich during the war. He always got on very well with everyone. He was a highly valued member of the Board of Deputies for many, many years and is universally known as "a real mensch". Together with his wife, they made an impressive and inspiring couple and Arieh did a great deal in furthering Mizrachi. We also worked together on the Labour Finance and Industry Group (LFIG).

He has never let his age get in the way of anything he undertook and has been a constant source of inspiration to me.

BOARD OF DEPUTIES OF BRITISH JEWS

It is a pleasure to be asked to add some words in tribute to Arieh Handler who is one of the last surviving people present when the Declaration of the State of Israel was signed on May 14th 1948. The extent of Arieh's achievements is only matched by his modesty in describing them.

I am delighted that in recent years his friends and family have persuaded him to give his account of his role in some of the most dramatic chapters in the history of our people. His account is interesting in itself but also for the insights it will provide for our own history.

Vivian Wineman (President)

DR. LIONEL KOPELOWITZ

I have known Arieh for 62 years. We first met in 1947 at the Bachad Hachshara in Thaxted, Essex, to which project he was totally committed. Indeed, the main road in the farm was called Handler Road.

At the same time, he was editing the weekly Bachad journal Chayenu, which was always an invaluable source of Bachad activities. I was in regular touch with him over the decades. He played a unique role at the Board of Deputies.

Arieh was always firm in conviction, forthright in speech, wise in counsel, staunch in support.

EFRAIM KRITZLER (KIBBUTZ LAVI)

Mr Arieh Handler arrived in Great Britain in 1938 and attended the last World Zionist Congress in Switzerland, which took place in 1939, before the outbreak of the Second World War.

As is well known, Great Britain enabled 10,000 children to come to its shores under the heading of "Kindertransport". Amongst these children, there were a large number of Jewish religious youth and Mr. Handler, with the help of the Jewish Refugee Committee of Great Britain, helped to absorb them in a number of Hachshara centres all over the United Kingdom.

In 1942 and 1943, Mr. Arieh Handler organised the many friends of the Religious Zionist Pioneer Movement into an organisation called The Bachad

Fellowship. In 1943 the Bachad Fellowship acquired a farm for young people, many of them born in England, who joined the Religious Pioneer Movement, Bachad (Brith Chalutzim Datim). This farm was situated in Thaxted, Essex. The movement's growth was partly achieved through the efforts of the Youth Leaders (madrichim) of Bachad who were active in the Bnei Akiva Movement (Religious Zionist Youth Movement) which set up branches all over the country.

Arieh's special strength and ability lay in convincing Jewish youth to prepare itself for life in Israel and in persuading the older members of Anglo-Jewry, amongst them many members of the academic community, the free professions and prominent business men, to support these efforts.

The Bachad movement grew into an organisation full of vitality which was appreciated by many sections of Anglo-Jewry and to this very day plays a major part in bringing thousands of religious olim to Israel.

BEN HELFGOTT MBE

I have known Arieh Handler from the time I was 16 years old when he visited the hostel where I lived with 30 other youngsters. The purpose of his visit was to encourage us to emigrate to Palestine.

His whole life was dedicated to the rescue of children, Russian Jews, and to the support of the State of Israel.

He is a man of the highest integrity, courage and wisdom who has left an indelible mark on many people.

RABBI ABRAHAM LEVY OBE

it has been my great pleasure to work with Arieh Handler for many years especially as co-trustee of the Montefiore Endowment, which has done so much to educate teachers and rabbis who spread Torah throughout the world.

It is for the remarkable success of Bnei Akiva in England that we owe a great debt to Arieh Handler. He has consistently succeeded over many years to present a Judaism which is fresh, wholesome and aware. He has managed to synthesise Torah, Zionism and secular culture in an exciting manner. Thank you Arieh for all that you have done for us.

RABBI DOW MARMUR

Because Arieh Handler is a man of faith, he is tolerant of those who worship God in other ways than his. Because his own religious commitment puts the care of God's creatures in the centre of spiritual life, he has been a supporter of politics with a social conscience both in Britain and Israel. Because for him the Faith of Israel, the People of Israel and the Land of Israel are all parts of being a Jew, he has been a life-long Zionist. Because schooled in the tradition that combines Torah with the way of the world he, together with his late wife, has been an ardent supporter of the arts.

It has been my privilege to encounter Arieh Handler in all these dimensions of his rich, rewarding life: as a partner in dialogue, despite our religious differences, as someone who shares his political interests, as a co-worker in the World Zionist Organization and as a visitor to his home in London and Jerusalem. It is my privilege to pay tribute to him and wish him the life of Moses – ad meah v'essrim.

JUNE JACOBS CBE

Arieh Handler has been a dear friend of mine for more years than I can remember. Going back to my involvement with Jewish Childs Day and the time that our Executive Committee joined forces with the Youth Aliyah Executive which was of course Arieh's organisation from the beginning.

After that arrangement finished some years later, happily for us Arieh remained on the JDC Board.

Arieh and I served on the Board of Deputies and we felt, in the early 1970s that there should be more communal activity on behalf of the Jews in the USSR. We finally got the support of the many communal organisations to form the National Council for Soviet Jewry and Arieh was then our Vice Chairman.

I am fortunate to have had such good friends as Arieh and his dear late wife Henni and I wish Arieh many more years of health and peace with his family in Israel.

WORLD MIZRACHI ORGANISATION

On my recent visit to Arieh Handler in Kiryat Moshe the taxi driver when I left remarked to me "you must have visited your Yedid Nefesh". It struck me that Arieh truly has been my soul mate in many years of service to our Jewish community and in our devotion to Israel.

Arieh's involvement in the creation of the State of Israel, his presence at the stirring founding ceremony in Tel Aviv, his deep involvement in Youth Aliyah, his leadership in the daring and successful efforts on behalf of Soviet Jewry are all of historic significance.

World Mizrachi, Bachad of England and World Bnei Akiva are proud to have Arieh in their leadership ranks.

Kurt Rothschild (Chairman)

ACKNOWLEDGMENTS

*I am so grateful to all those who helped with the production of
this short tribute to Arieh Handler, his sons Danny and Gaby,
Rabbi Professor Marc Saperstein, the late Israel Finestein Q. C.,
Jeremy Dresner, Leo Allen and all those
who contributed tributes.*

*A special thanks to Sir Martin Gilbert PC, CBE, D.Litt.
for his Introduction and to Chief Rabbi Lord Jonathan Sacks
for his Foreword.*

*Erika Valensi, Michele Peled and Aliza Evron, all of Tel Aviv
University, worked so long and so hard on the drafts,
documents and photographs. My grateful thanks to them.*

*Without the expertise of graphic designer Chris Smith this book
would not have seen the light of day.*

*And of course, many thanks to the late Joseph Finklestone who
began a comprehensive biography of Arieh but who sadly
passed away long before its completion.*

AUBREY ROSE